HOW WE DO BUSINESS

CLYDE'S PRIMER FOR BEATING THE ODDS IN THE RESTAURANT BUSINESS

J. GARRETT GLOVER

Brick Tower Press
New York

Brick Tower Press
New York
1230 Park Avenue, 9a
New York, New York 101
Bricktower@aol.com • www.BrickTowerPress.com

Printed by J. T. Colby & Company, Inc. New York.

How We Do Business: Clyde's Primer for Beating the Odds in the Restaurant Business

Glover, J. Garrett

Library of Congress Cataloging in Publication Data

Glover, J. Garrett

How We Do Business: Clyde's Primer for Beating the Odds in the Restaurant Business / by J. Garrett Glover

p. cm.

ISBN 978-1-883283-86-5

1. Biography & Autobiography—Business. 2. Business & Economics: Industries—Food Industry. 3. Cooking—General. I. Title

2013

CIP

June 2013

Artwork, illustrations, graphics and photographs for How We Do Business were commissioned or generated by Clyde's between

1963 and 2013 for purposes of illustration, advertising, marketing, promotions and/or decoration; these elements were exported

from either the company's archives or the private collections of its officers. Special thanks to Sally Davidson, Ginger Laytham and

Maureen Hirsch for providing and granting access to the images. Acknowledgments to Ron Blunt for architectural photography,

Charma Le Edmonds and Shelter Studios for food photography, and Tim Olive of Tim Olive Productions for the portraits of fishermen

and farmer. Copyright for the front cover illustration: 1980 Clyde's Investment Corporation.

Design services by Mike Stromberg at Great American Art. Creative by J. Garrett Glover.

CONTENTS

4

PREFACE

How We Do Business is a primer. And as primers go, broadly speaking, *How We Do Business* introduces a subject of study by presenting the subject in its most rudimentary elements. Recall the alphabet book, a quintessential primer. Similarly, this primer exposes the ABCs of a perennially bankable restaurant company, Clyde's Restaurant Group, headquartered in Washington, DC.

2013 marks Clyde's Golden Anniversary, fifty years beating the odds in the tough, fickle business of running profitable restaurants, arguably the most strident, riskiest legit business known to man. Clyde's intrepid performance and success over fifty years make theirs a noteworthy story. Even more so, their success makes for an awesome case study of how out-of-the-box thinking and a modicum of sophistication can transform a meat-and-potatoes business…or any business, for that matter.

Clyde's opened its first restaurant in 1963, at 3236 M Street, NW, in Washington's notorious Georgetown neighborhood. Over these fifty years, the medium-sized, privately owned business opened fourteen restaurants at eleven properties in the District of Columbia, Maryland and Virginia, the smallest a cozy Georgetown University rathskeller, the largest a 37,000-square-foot multiplex restaurant and live-music venue two blocks from the White House. In its first year, the Georgetown store grossed approximately $250,000; in 2011, *Restaurants and Institutions* listed the company's historic DC landmark, Old Ebbitt Grill, as the fourth highest-grossing restaurant in the country at $26 million. 2012 to 2013 has the company on pace to gross $130 million; no peanuts for a regional independent that, unlike national restaurant chains, wants nothing to do with cookie-cutter storefronts.

Yet, the most significant feat to date in the company's fifty years is that the operators have never closed a restaurant. Nor have they turned over ownership or franchised. All fifteen locations are still open and the company is profitable. A staggering feat considering the odds: "…one in four restaurants close or change ownership within their first year of business. Over three years, that number rises to three in five." Not a single fatality in fifty years, impressive for a small business jointly owned and operated by two partners. "How do they do it?" people often ask.

To answer that question is what this primer is about. And the answer comes in dialogue straight from the mouths of those in the know: Sally Davidson, chairman of the board and surviving spouse of the founder and majority owner, Stuart Carleton Davidson; John Gibb Laytham, Stuart's and now Sally's vested partner, co-owner and CEO; Ginger Laytham, John's wife and senior executive officer to the president, CEO and chairman; and Tom Moyor, prooidont. Although oditod for print, tho dialoguo of these four brassy characters has been left in the raw. Clyde's ubiquitous culture casts an indelible charisma, one that very much reflects the character of the people who run it. To hear these voices raw is to know Clyde's intimately, to intercept a sense of why Clyde's has been so successful, a sense that would be lost if translated into prose. There is no BS, no hype in these voices; they ring cleanly making it clear that Clyde's is about sound business and authenticity in everything they do.

As with many primers, there are no chapters per se in Clyde's primer, only sequentially placed sections presenting the ABCs of Clyde's MO. The section headings are suggestive of the subject: a facet of Clyde's history ("A Harvard Grad in a Backwater Town Seeking an Upper East Side Bar Meets a Hoya Towhead") or an integral company proposition ("Inconsistency In Management Is Really Bad For Morale") or a strategy about food product ("No More Melons from Another Hemisphere. Or, You Can't Shine Shit"). The beauty of primers is that they can be read front to back, back to front or from the center out. The Clyde's primer is no exception. Its design allows the reader to read the material in whatever order the reader pleases. Start at the front and read back, scan the "Contents" for a heading that catches the eye, or casually flip through the book.

Placed throughout are the interstitials, "Words To Live By" and "Beating the Odds Means...." Each interstitial is an adage that in and of itself expresses a general truth or axiom about how Clyde's does business. Stuart C. Davidson has been regaled far and wide for his quip, "It's more fun to eat in a saloon than drink in a restaurant." But, like the other interstitials, this quip is more than a one-liner. It catches a fundamental concept that differentiated Clyde's approach to the restaurant/saloon business early on, an approach that has been widely adopted by ersatz Clyde's saloons.

A brief history of Clyde's Restaurant Group has been added at the back of the primer as a reference for those who want to read more about the locations mentioned in the dialogues. In keeping with the theme "how we do business," the short history is both a chronicle of the restaurants and a chronicle of Clyde's corporate policies effectively put to work.

No primer is worth its weight in gold without super illustrations. In fact, the original idea behind the book was to publish not a primer but a glossy coffee-table edition packed with gorgeous photos of Clyde's properties. There is every good reason to show off the sublime design and museum-quality furnishings and fixtures, decorative hardware and glass, the commissioned artwork and *objets d'art* that punch up Clyde's restaurants. "Creating an experience like you're going somewhere else" – to quote John Laytham – figures largely in Clyde's scrupulous efforts to transform exterior and interior design and ambiance into transcendent experiences for the customer.

Furthermore, Clyde's looks at its FF&F not only as payoffs for customers looking for attractive places to dine but also as real investments that gain value over time. "It's nice to see things you buy actually appreciate rather than everything depreciating," says Laytham. The photos, images and illustrations included here have been selected because each in some way illustrates a milestone practice or principle behind Clyde's winning formula.

A final note about *How We Do Business*. Primers inform, that is their primary purpose; but primers also entertain using humor and delight, again recall the alphabet book. Reading the dialogues here, it should become clear that wit, humor, joy and fun are part and parcel of the Clyde's experience, doing things "in the spirit of having a good time," as Tom Meyer says it. The primer intends to show this "spirit" and implores readers to roll with the good times when they see them coming. Read on. *Laissez les bon temps rouler.*

NON MEA CULPA

"I don't know of too many restaurants who have been around for fifty years or too many restaurant companies who haven't closed a restaurant."

John G. Laytham, Clyde's Restaurant Group

"…about one in four restaurants close or change ownership within their first year of business. Over three years, that number rises to three in five."

http://www.businessweek.com/stories/2007-04-16/the-restaurant-failure-mythbusinessweek-business- news-stock-market-and-financial-advice

Restaurant Company Org Chart
Default Public View

Board & Corporate Management
Restaurant Management
Suppliers & Trades
Line Employees
Customers

Restaurant Company Org Chart
Clyde's View

Customers
Line Employees
Suppliers & Trades
Restaurant Management
Board & Corporate Management

 **BEATING THE ODDS MEANS ...**

...DON'T FOCUS ON THE BEANS BUT WHAT CREATES THE BEANS.

JOHN   To me making money in the restaurant business is kind of a byproduct of doing what is really important correctly, which is taking care of the customer, taking care of your employees and making sure they have what they need to serve the customers correctly. If you're focused basically on counting the beans and not on what creates the beans, you end up not making it for the most part. I've seen it happen over and over again.

11

BLUE LAWS, BLUE CITY, RED HOT SOCIETY, RED HOT CLYDE'S

The District of Columbia's blue laws, particularly those of the early 20th century regulating the sale and consumption of alcohol (e.g., hard liquor could only be consumed sitting at a table, not standing at a bar), raised a drab blue persona on an otherwise brilliant and forward-looking city. The stigma created by these antiquated blue laws debunked the Nation's Capital; next to red-hot societies like Manhattan, DC came across as a subfusc backwater town, a deplorable identity Washingtonians fled from but one that Eastern Airlines gladly profited by. The Eastern Air Shuttle between DC and New York carried a weekly cargo of Washingtonians fleeing their city for cocktails and a cheeseburger at P.J. Clarke's Third Avenue bar or a Sunday champagne brunch at the Plaza.

Relief from DC's draconian blue laws came in 1962, when a bill slid unimpeded across President Kennedy's desk legalizing the sale of liquor to patrons bellying up to bars in the District. Taking note was Georgetowner Stuart C. Davidson, one of Eastern's frequent flyers to P.J. Clarke's bar. When President Kennedy signed the belly-up bill, there came to Stuart a startlingly momentous epiphany that would shake up the hospitality industry in DC for at least the next fifty years. "A bar in Washington could do very well," Stuart muttered to himself.

SALLY When Stuart opened Clyde's, it was because the liquor laws changed in 1962. He was at a turning point in his life and trying to decide whether he wanted to go back to New York or Boston, and get a job again in investment banking, which is what he was doing, which he hated. But anyway, he read or heard that the liquor laws had changed and nobody had done anything about it. So he took over this biker bar in Georgetown and opened Clyde's in 1963. Stuart knew exactly what Washington needed.

"It's more fun to eat in a saloon than drink in a restaurant."

Stuart C. Davidson

A Harvard Grad in a Backwater Town Seeking an Upper East Side Bar Meets a Hoya Towhead

Stuart Carleton Davidson, a Harvard grad, Army Air Force pilot, heir to the National Cash Register Company fortune, a bon vivant Georgetowner, apostle to the faith that "It's more fun to eat in a saloon than drink in a restaurant," believed with heart, soul and palate that he was not alone in DC thinking that a Celtic watering hole, like New York's P.J. Clarke's, was a sorely missed amusement in Capital City.

SALLY That's what he kind of patterned his original Clyde's after, P.J. Clarke's. We talked about why the name Clyde. Stuart was of Scottish descent. He liked things Scottish. He always had a kilt or two. He wanted a short name that people could remember. I think one of the other finalist names was Floyd's. It came finally down to Clyde's, after the River Clyde in Scotland. But what it really came down to was Clyde's, a Scottish name and the "C" makes a fabulous logo. Clyde's was a short name and the "C" makes a fabulous logo. And it does!

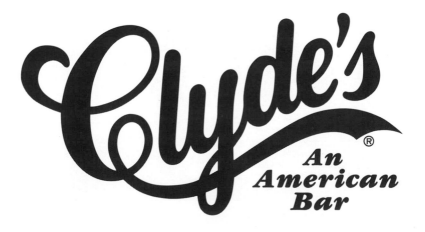

DC was prime for an Upper East Side Manhattan-style bar. What better neighborhood to put it in than tony historic Georgetown, home for seven years to John and Jackie Kennedy and their Camelot cronies before the Kennedys moved into the White House in January 1961? For some time, Stuart had had his eye on B&J's Restaurant, a biker dive on M Street. When the landlord refused to renew Bernie and Joe's lease, Stuart jumped on the opportunity.

SALLY He knew that's what Washington needed. And he was totally amazed that nobody had taken advantage of the change in the liquor laws. Stuart had a good eye. He knew what he was talking about. Clyde's was such an immediate, huge success even though he didn't know the business. Who has that kind of window now? Nobody.

GINGER Stuart opened Clyde's of Georgetown on August 12, 1963. He knew there was a void in Georgetown, in the city, for the type of restaurant that Clyde's is. He saw that void and he filled it. John didn't join Stuart until the next March.

John Gibb Laytham, a bright towhead from near Pottstown, PA, and a freshman at Georgetown's School of Foreign Service, walked into Clyde's looking for a part-time job to earn pocket change. Stuart hired John first as a dishwasher and later promoted him to a busboy.

SALLY John was working here as a busboy, then a waiter, a bartender, and so, fairly early on, Stuart recognized that this guy understands the business. John had become a manager and he'd worked his way through every job and Stuart offered him a minority partnership. Well, John thought about it for a while. Stuart was about to say, "Well, if you're not interested, you're not interested." It took John a long time to decide whether to do it or not, and his wife at the time, Janet, said, "Do it!"

Stuart got rid of his former partner, got a grip on the business, got good people like John involved and fired all the crooked bartenders. Stuart was an investment banker. He really didn't know anything about the service industry. But he was right. Clyde's was exactly what Washington needed. Clyde's was jammed from day one.

THE PARTNERSHIP, THAT'S GONNA BE YOUR LAST MEMORY, OF HAVING A WONDERFUL DINNER AND SHOOTING THE SHIT ABOUT ALL THE CRAZY THINGS THAT WENT ON OVER THE YEARS

Arguably one can make the case that the nature of, the quality of, the partnership between Stuart and John was instrumental in Clyde's phenomenal long-term success.

GINGER   Oh, there's no question about it. If the two partners did not share the same vision of what the restaurant group should be, it would have been very difficult.

JOHN   I would say one of the things my dealings with my partner did was help shape my view of how business should be done. You know, there's this great view of people in the restaurant business that they go and take money out of the cash register or under the table and do all these kinds of things. Stuart would never do something like that. Nor would I. Because if you expect your employees to be honest, you have to be impeccably honest yourself.

   I learned a lot of basic business principles from Stuart. Always doing things well if you're going to do them at all. Always making sure that you have the capital necessary to do what you're planning on doing. Stuart always understood the whole idea of taking care of customers in one way or another.

TOM   What Stuart gave me was courage. He was like, if we're gonna do it, do it right. We got the money to do it. We're not gonna do anything half-ass. We're gonna do it and we're gonna do it right and we're gonna be fine.

John   I mentioned in Stuart's eulogy about, you know, he was sort of a tight-fisted Scotsman in one way, but he always wanted to do things exactly right. A Scotsman that doesn't like wasting a penny particularly, although he loved beautiful things. He was a collector of all sorts of artwork.

SALLY   He bought Henry Moores, Calders and Archipenkos way back in the '50s. He really had an eye for things that were done well. And he appreciated that and supported that whether it was in a restaurant or in an art gallery.

Stuart Davidson

John Laytham

Clyde's

3236 M. Street NW

JOHN Stuart always kind of hammered home if you're going to build something then build it well. You don't really want to have to come back and redo it in two years or three years. So it came from Stuart as much as anyone in the company, insisting on always spending the extra money but having it right. We certainly got the spending money part right!

SALLY Stuart had perhaps a good overall financial view, you know, a big overall financial view. John has an amazing capacity for detail as well as the financial view, but an amazing capacity for detail. Together, they made *the* perfect partnership.

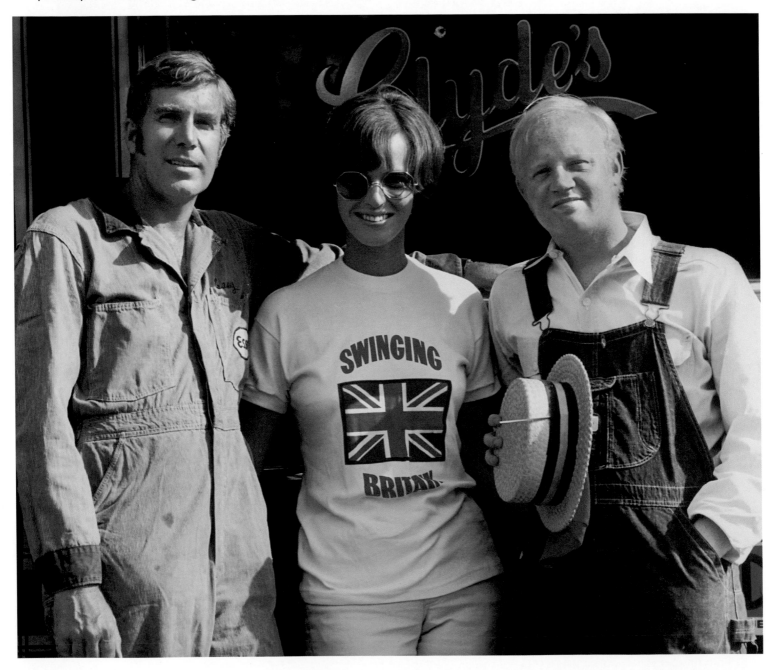

GINGER Both Stuart and John appreciated quality very much. And I don't think they ever, ever would lower their standards. They'd rather not do something than lower their standards and put out something second rate. But they were also fiscally conservative. They never took risks that they didn't think were appropriate.

JOHN Well, it's nice to see things you buy actually appreciate rather than everything depreciating.

GINGER Meeting Stuart when he was still in college, John certainly picked up a lot from Stuart. That exposure really molded John's development, his reach for excellence. And, ultimately, Stuart and John got on the same page about everything having to do with business.

SALLY Stuart set a very high standard and I think it has been maintained over the years.

JOHN I mean he was involved in everything. What artists we chose, when we built a new restaurant, what direction we were going with the décor. He was involved with the meetings with the architect, and so to that extent, you know, Stuart, particularly in those areas, had a lot of input. We talked about what we were going to do or what I wanted to do but usually he'd say, "If that's what you think, go ahead and do it." Stuart gave me a lot of freedom to make changes, to implement new ideas and programs. And I always felt he was there supporting me and giving me the opportunity to do what I thought was necessary.

GINGER John could always rely on Stuart to bounce ideas off of. John knew that he could always get an honest answer from Stuart. Stuart was very candid, you know!

JOHN Which is what I try to do with all the people who are now involved with me.

TOM I thought Stuart gave people courage to act boldly. He let you swing big. And I have to say John took that and took it to a new level. And, you know, this company has never operated from fear.

GINGER Stuart saw the vision of what was needed but I never heard that he wanted to be the day-to-day operations person. I don't think he saw his role as being that. Stuart hired people to manage the restaurant. He was the investor who owned it and wanted to hire the best possible people to manage the operations and the kitchens and so forth. Stuart gave John a lot of leeway, a lot of free reign on the operational side of things. And John never did anything without talking to Stuart and getting his point of view.

JOHN   I think over time Stuart just gained confidence in my abilities and therefore gave me a tremendous amount of freedom to make decisions. As I say, it wasn't that he was concerned about what I did or what we did. I think that might be kind of an unusual thing, the fact that he gave me freedom the way he did. I think my role was to recognize what was necessary and to make sure we had it.

TOM   I'd say that what those two had in common was they were introverted dudes. They were kind of, in a way, both kind of waspy, you know. They were heavy cats and they were not afraid and they would take the risks and never look back. They were up there to hit homeruns, not bunt their way to first base. You know, they were like swingin'. And if we made mistakes, which are inevitable you know, I can say I never heard John say, "I told you so."

 And they played off each other. They had a real appreciation, respect for everybody working for them. I mean, that's the way I would describe their kind of partnership.

JOHN   All that kind of went before us had a lot to do with the fact that we've been able to create wonderful things. We kind of created a situation that people really wanted *us* to be the person that did their project.

SALLY   Stuart knew when you put out really good things, *really* good, the public will recognize and appreciate it. And they really do recognize it.

TOM   Yeah, like when we'd be picking out salt and pepper shakers, or if you were gonna get a frame, Stuart'd say, "Always pick the bigger one. If you're gonna make an error, make your error be larger than smaller." Which is totally right. Like a chandelier, people want to pick what they're used to in their homes and Stuart says, "We need like a twelve-foot chandelier." Stuart was wild, man. That's a whole book.

In a primer that intends to be a case study, a tell-it-like-it-is case study, of a successful independent restaurant company, it would be an unforgivable deceit not to confess up front that many, if not most, successful restaurateurs are eccentric in one way or another and to some degree. They're just a very different breed. Try to hide this and the book would not be credible with peers and colleagues. It takes an eccentric to be successful in the restaurant business. Opening this door with no apologies, Stuart's eccentricity brought a lot to Clyde's table.

TOM   I mean, Stuart was eccentric. I don't really want to say it 'cause it's such a cliché, but, you know, that whole kind of out-of-the-box thinking. One of my first dialogues with Stuart was he had these two negatives. They were fairly large negatives of artwork. And he was thinking about buying them for when you go down the front stairs at the Ebbitt. So he says, "Which one do you like, young man?" So he shows one to me, this is like a big lady with like big breasts. And he shows me this other one, it's the white woman, white bear rugs, the naked lady with the bear and the parrot, you know. So, I'm like, is this like a trick question? I said, "Well, I think I like the green one, Stuart." "Well, I like the big girl, too, but I think this one might be better because I think more people will be interested in seeing the parrot." Well, okay, Stuart, can I get out of here now?

JOHN   In a way, that kind of eccentricity, whatever, just gives you a broader view of the world. It kind of introduced a whole different level of sophistication in saloons, in a way.

TOM   Certainly a level of taste and sophistication that I wasn't hip to at the time, you know.

JOHN   I mean, we had single malt scotches back when mostly everybody in the city and certainly everyone across the river was drinking nothing but bourbon, you know. Scotch was sort of part of the city growing up from a sleepy little southern town to being a pretty sophisticated city.

TOM   Stuart brought a big time business attitude to a business that was really run out of cigar boxes at the time. He brought like a real business sense to a mom-and-pop industry.

SALLY   Well, Stuart's eccentricity became more creative and constructive after he quit drinking. All of that eccentricity combined with drinking was not a good combo, to say the least. It's kind of interesting how he quit drinking.
   We were at his sister Mary's house for Thanksgiving. And Stuart and I and Mary's son, Byron, were in watching the football game. And we were drinking champagne. Stuart took a half-full glass of champagne, set it down on the table and said, "I'm not going to drink anymore." And that was it. He never had a drink again.
   Wow! He looked back on his life. Not maybe that moment, but in general, looked back on his life and what the drinking had produced, contributed to, was all not good and so, that day, that afternoon, that afternoon...he made the decision. He didn't' drink anything after that. Somebody asked him one time, "Do you miss drinking?" And he said, "The only thing I miss is really good red wine." That was an amazing thing.

JOHN   But, you know, I think some of the best restaurants we've done have been since Stuart died. But it was what I learned and what we'd done together in the years before he died that made it possible to think and create the kinds of things we have ended up doing since then.

So even though Stuart's not here, without what we've learned and I've learned from him and what we learned together, it would be impossible to do Tower Oaks, Gallery Place and the Farm and The Hamilton. All of which were big projects and all of which we got in since Stuart died.

TOM Stuart and John, they were like saloon dudes. They knew what it means to sit down and, you know, belly up, what it means to have a great saloon. And Stuart, I think, took the Upper East Side New York saloon, the original Clyde's, and John said, "I'm gonna put unique and wonderful food to this and that's what I'm gonna do." And that's why he busted out loose from the rest of the gang. He said I'm gonna put the Omelette Room in. I'm gonna bust this open. I'm gonna do some of the food that this town hasn't seen. I'm gonna pay attention to the casual. You could argue Stuart and John invented the casual dining segment almost, you know. Before that you ate in a diner, a hotel or a fancy French restaurant. I mean, you couldn't get a decent meal in a saloon.

GINGER Stuart and John had a shared common business sense. And a great respect for each other. I remember that, and it was very dear, Harvard had a cocktail party and dinner in the atrium of the Old Ebbitt Grill to honor Stuart. They wanted to give Stuart an award and for Stuart to give a little speech. And so Stuart asked John if he would go with him. And John said yes, of course. So they both wound up speaking at the event and after it was over, Stuart gave the award to John. And he said, "I think you really earned this."

But, I remember John came home and he was beyond touched, beyond touched. Stuart always recognized John's contribution to the company and in so many ways he always let that be known. But, it's a little something like that that really kind of spoke volumes.

JOHN One of the things, by the way, that it was with Stuart was that even after forty years, we could have a good time together. The last night I saw Stuart was when Ginger and I were at his house with Sally. Ginger and Sally had flown up stone crab claws and key lime pie from Joe's Stone Crab in Florida, and then we just had a great night telling tales. I was going to Nantucket and he was going on a cruise to the Arctic Circle and we just had a really, really great night together. And my memory of him was – and we talked about his eccentricity – was him sitting there with the bird on his shoulder when we left.

GINGER I think the bird's name was Jorito. Jorito was flying around the neighborhood, clearly

24

someone's bird that had been lost, and they took it in and made every effort to find the owner, but to no avail. So there was Stuart sort of beaming with that bird sitting on his shoulder eating stone crabs.

JOHN   He was so proud of the fact that the bird only liked him and didn't like Sally 'cause she had all the birds you know.

GINGER   Thinking about that last dinner always brings me to tears. Stuart and John really did like each other very much. They truly admired each other.

SALLY   Theirs was such a genuine friendship. I think they really cared about each other. I know they did. And they built a wonderful business relationship but, you know, they really got along. I think they understood each other.

GINGER   They were very different people, had different interests. Stuart was skiing and kayaking and John couldn't get enough golf. I'm sure they disagreed on things at times, came at things in a different way, but at the end of the day, they always walked in lockstep, supporting each other. Such a long collaboration. That's an amazing partnership.

JOHN   You know, it's just kind of nice after being partners with somebody for forty years that that's gonna be your last memory, of having a wonderful dinner and shooting the shit about all the crazy things that went on over the years.

I'm Going to Have to Get a Real Job Eventually

JOHN Stuart, for the longest time, kind of viewed Clyde's as kind of an amusement. A place where he could go and drink and do whatever he wanted. He'd been thrown out of a number of bars in Georgetown. So I don't think he ever viewed Clyde's as something he was ever really going to make money from.

SALLY It took several years, I mean, really several years, seven to ten years, before Stuart accepted that this was a real job. Because the way he was raised you were either a doctor, a lawyer, a banker. His father was a general and he was an Army brat. He went to Harvard and Harvard Business School. You didn't go into the service industry. When there was Georgetown, the old Old Ebbitt, Columbia, Tysons, when it got to be four or five restaurants, he was still thinking, "I'm going to have to get a real job eventually."

It amazed me how long it took him to just accept the fact that he enjoyed it and it was successful and that he didn't have to continue thinking that he would sell it and get a real job again.

IT'LL TEAR THE PLACE APART

JOHN The first three or four years of my being involved with Clyde's, my focus was just how successful could I make Clyde's. It really never had made any money.

We were so successful by changing the menu, changing the food, emphasizing brunches, changing the service in the place, that within three years we'd gone from $250,000 to over a million dollars in sales, which is a 400% increase in three years. Stuart said Clyde's cost him $100,000 but half of that was stolen. It should have cost only $50,000. So I remember going up to Stuart and being all proud of the fact that we did over a million dollars and said, "Stuart, I just wanted to let you know that we went over a million dollars."

And he said, "I don't think I want to do that. It'll tear the place apart."

GROWING THE COMPANY...ONLY IN HAVANA

With Clyde's purchase of the Old Ebbitt Grill downtown on F Street, the opening of Clyde's in Columbia, Maryland, and building Clyde's of Tysons in Northern Virginia, Stuart and John prove their mettle now successfully developing and running multiple restaurants. Clyde's formula for "How We Do Business" begins to materialize. Yet, what's interesting is that Clyde's growth and ensuing success then and now were almost more fortuitous than intentional.

JOHN   Well, I guess I looked at it as growing the company over time, in a kind of calculated, unrushed sort of way. In other words, I didn't feel we had to open a restaurant every year or every other year but it was more dependent of finding a location we really liked and finding a deal that really made sense. I've never had any specific goal about how big the company should be or how big it should get, or how quickly it should get big. The only place I'd really like to do one is in Havana. I just think it's a fabulous place. It'd be a cool place to have a restaurant.

   And I never wanted to build something you stamped out either. To be doing something nationwide, you're building twenty-five restaurants a year, you're basically having some model you're stamping out everywhere. I mean, none of the Clyde's restaurants are the same. They're all different. You don't feel like when you go into Clyde's you're going into a chain, as such, because none of them look like any of the other ones. I don't think.

LOCATION. NOT JUST A PLACE TO GO AND GET A DRINK OR A HAMBURGER

"Location, location, location. Location is everything." Stuart C. Davidson

GINGER Location, location, location, that reminds me. The Chairman of the Board of Goldman Sachs had done some study on the Clyde's Restaurant Group and wanted to come down and tour our properties and have John talk to him about the industry and so forth. He looked at John and asked, "So who does all your property selection for you? What company have you hired to do that?"

And John just looked at him and said, "Well, we do that."

The chairman was baffled, just like, "Really? You don't have professionals? There are companies, whole companies, that's what they specialize in. Well, what criteria do you use?"

And John said, you know, that he and Stuart just had a second sense about neighborhoods, like Tysons or Reston. Obviously, people come to us with opportunities weekly but those opportunities have always been reviewed by us.

JOHN We've always looked for a place where there was a real need for what we wanted to do. I mean the original Clyde's, Stuart always loved things like P.J. Clarke's in New York, and saloons in New York, and yet there was not a single place like that in Washington. So there was obviously a need for it. When we went to Columbia....

GINGER Columbia, being on a lakefront in a planned community.

JOHN There was nothing like a Clyde's of Columbia. When we went to Tysons Corner, there was nothing like a Clyde's really in Tysons Corner.

GINGER And Reston, there was no town center. There was no Reston downtown. And to be the first restaurant to sign and to demand that corner, right at the fountain and right next door to where the Pavilion is now, Stuart and John could see the vision of what Reston Town Center would become and what it needed.

JOHN We thought we were basically fulfilling a need in a particular community that we opened a restaurant in.

"Fulfilling a need" comes up often at Clyde's when talking about location selection. Knowing the need may be a spectral second sense but it is also an intuition about the most elemental, palpable experience in the service industry, if not in all businesses.

JOHN It's been a question whether the market is big enough to warrant one of our restaurants in the sense of what the competition is. I mean, that's one of the things that we've always tried to do: is not look at a restaurant just as a place to go and get a drink or a hamburger but as the idea of creating an experience for people. And that's what there wasn't a lot of in those days and that's what to some degree there still isn't even a lot of today: creating an experience for people.

WORDS TO LIVE BY

"What I think happens to a lot of restaurateurs is they focus on the bottom line only and not on the customers."

John G. Laytham

BEATING THE ODDS MEANS ...

...P = V + S

Profitability = Value + Service

"Managing costs and percentages have little bearing on increased sales. Sales are a variable of value and service; the value of the product and the level of service as perceived by the customer. Those businesses that are perceived as "having value" normally experience repeat customers, increased sales and growth. Value, then, is not a commodity, not an article that can be traded; value is the sum total of the customers' perception of the operation, of the services they receive. Given the correlation between profitability and customers' perception, superior value and superior service are critical to the success of the restaurant."

Excerpt from *Clyde's Management Manual* by J. Garrett Glover

CREATING AN EXPERIENCE, LIKE YOU'RE GOING SOMEWHERE ELSE

JOHN Our formula has been to build really pretty large restaurants. I think one of the things we've been really successful doing over the years is breaking up spaces and, even in a large restaurant, making them feel somewhat intimate. And that also gives us a chance to change the décor to some degree from room to room. You're not committed to having just one décor for the whole place.

If you look at all of our restaurants, we just don't have giant rooms. That was what somebody was just talking to me about last week and saying, "We know that restaurant (The Hamilton) is 37,000 square feet, but it doesn't feel like it's 37,000 square feet."

Going out really needs to be an experience for people. I really mean that. The treatment that you get from the employees, the feeling of the restaurant, is it comfortable, is it warm, is the food good, is it consistent, is the ambiance right, you know? I mean there are so many things that go into creating a great experience for people and I think making it a constant objective to meet those criteria is critical to whether or not you're successful in the long run. And whether you get repeat business.

Getting repeat business is kind of the most critical thing in the business, the fact that you can't afford to have anyone leave your restaurant unhappy. And you need to do whatever you need to do to make sure that doesn't happen. Not that you'll never make mistakes, not that you'll never have problems. But, you know, some of our best customers and most loyal customers are people who have had a problem at the restaurant the first time they were there and the way we handled it was part of them becoming regular long-term customers.

One of the reasons we end up spending as much money as we do on the restaurants is to make it feel like you're going somewhere else. You're not going out to just get a burger, although probably for a lot of our customers that's the way they look at it, but the whole idea of creating a warm, comfortable place, an environment to enjoy your night out.

32

It is important to point out that John here refers to an "environment" and not the "interior décor" when talking about the customer experience. The idea of creating an environment morphed into something like a habitat when Clyde's built the Mark Center restaurant. Stuart and John fabricated five different habitat vignettes in Mark Center's three dining rooms and two bars.

JOHN I mean Clyde's at Mark Center was the scariest of all the new locations that we did. It certainly wasn't an "A" location and two restaurants had failed there. But we just felt that if we created the right kind of environment out there that people would come. And they certainly have. We did the Chesapeake Room and we did the Adirondacks Room. We did the crew thing, the sports thing. We did the sailing thing. We did the Nantucket Room. It was just creating kind of fun vignettes of places we liked and things we liked.

   The whole idea of going out is it should be fun. It shouldn't just be walking in to feed your face. And that's part of the whole idea of it being a place that you like actually to hang out in when you're not working and you're not at home. You know, what the whole idea of the third place is.

Ray Oldenburg introduces the idea of the "third place" in *The Great Good Place* (1989) to describe public places where people spontaneously and regularly meet socially outside the home and work place. Third places, whether a hair salon, pub, coffee house, town square, etc., are more often than not the heart of a community's social life. Throughout DC, Northern Virginia and Maryland, Clyde's restaurants and bars have been for fifty years considered landmark community gathering places: "Meet me at Clyde's."

...THIRD PLACE IS A GOOD THING.

BEATING THE ODDS MEANS ...

JOHN There are a lot of people who come regularly and go to a number of our restaurants regularly. They view us as their kind of place when they're not home or at work, that's where they are. The third place.

CUSTOMERS DON'T THINK ABOUT AMBIANCE. THEY JUST KIND OF KNOW IT

JOHN If I walk around one of our restaurants and there are things that need to be replaced and they haven't been replaced; or there's a rug that's worn or they're obviously missing like eight or ten bar stools that they haven't reordered; or if the lighting was wrong in the old days — it would drive me crazy — and seeing management — we drum that into people's head, managers are on the floor in these restaurants; or if I go in and the music's not right — it's either too loud or it's the wrong kind of music — then somebody hasn't been listening in training about how well the place is being kept up or how clean the kitchen looks. You know, customers don't think about ambiance, they just kind of know it, whether it's comfortable or not comfortable.

BEATING THE ODDS MEANS ...

...NEVER LET ANYTHING REALLY DOMINATE THE RESTAURANT.

JOHN   We've never let anything we do dominate the restaurant. I've seen so many places define themselves either by how loud they play the music or the kind of music they play and it really limits their clientele. You can go into our restaurants and see a couple that's twenty-one-years old and you'll see a couple that's seventy-years old. And they both feel comfortable. We've always done that. We've never let anything really dominate and therefore limit the clientele of our restaurants.

A KICKER IN EVERY DEAL

JOHN It always seemed to me that restaurants in theory are scary businesses period, right? In terms of its success rate and everything else? And I just always felt that there ought to be something in the restaurant deals you make that kind of protects you if you made a miscalculation. There should be a kicker in every deal you make. It's important. And to go way out on a limb without some kind of protection seems to me to be not prudent. I just always considered that critical.

Sometimes it's better not to make a deal and not to do something than it is to do something just to do it. In other words, if I'm not comfortable with the restaurant deal, I'd rather not build the restaurant than make something that I didn't feel protected in.

When I say I always felt there has to be a real kicker in any deal you make; I think you can see that we do do that. And I think one of the reasons that we've been able to make these really good deals over the years is because of the quality of the places we've created and our long-term success in running them. For the landlord to make a serious commitment to you as his tenant, I think you have to be able to convince him that they're going to get a product that's going to be an asset to their property. An asset to what they're trying to accomplish overall.

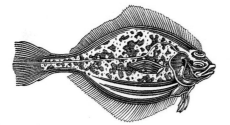 *GROWING THE ORGANIZATION. YOU JUST CAN'T DO IT ALL YOURSELF. OR, WHEN BY THE SEAT OF THE PANTS NO LONGER WORKS*

JOHN   It was just sort of an interesting thing that all growing companies go through. You have to make a transition at some point from running it by the seat of your pants to realizing that you really need some corporate management.

I was looking at it as it was kind of my responsibility to oversee all of whatever we did and kind of run them. I was also involved in supervising the construction of new restaurants. And, when I could go to manager meetings, I could sort of infuse my own views on basically every decision that was made at every restaurant. In other words, I was there to either say yes or no or to counsel people on how to handle personnel or how to handle this and that. But, you know, you just can't do it all yourself. And so how to grow and add management to running the company without bankrupting the company? It was just kind of a step-by-step, "What do I need now?"

HE'S AN ASSHOLE. HE'S THIS, HE'S THAT

JOHN   By the time we finished Columbia, I was starting to have problems with people because I wasn't there. At the same time, we were opening Tysons, which was the biggest restaurant we've ever opened and was awfully scary when interest rates went from 8% to the prime rate at 21 and we were paying 2% over prime on our construction loan. We put up two million of our own and it's good we borrowed only four million instead of eight million. I don't know what would have happened if we didn't have the two million. But four million at 23%, I think it was sixty or seventy thousand a month that we were paying in interest, which was a lot of money with the place not open. Believe it or not, back in 1980, that was a lot of money. And the opening was delayed three months by a strike by the air conditioning company because they had to lower the air conditioning equipment in through the roof of the Atrium. So they couldn't close in the Atrium or put in the woodwork, any of the woodwork, until Trane's strike was over and we could get that in. It was an interesting time, let's put it that way. It was a scary time.

I got worried about things like what one manager said, "I don't like working for that manager. He's an asshole." He's this, he's that. When I wasn't there, it's when the weaknesses started showing up, that people were out on their own going their own ways, doing their own things. The company was just getting too big. I decided, "Well, I guess it's time we're going to have to start looking at doing something differently." So that began the reorganizing of the company.

That was sort of the birth of the idea of analyzing what the company was all about, the whole idea of what makes us successful, what do we need to do to be successful? What's the role of management? How can management be more consistent?

Clyde's Training Center, 1987. As Clyde's expanded, Stuart and John acknowledged the risk of losing control over the consistency of product, service and management practices in the individual restaurants. The owners decided to take primary classroom training for service and management personnel out of the units and run it through a corporate training center in Georgetown; lessons from the center would then be reinforced back in the units where trainees worked actual shifts with mentors. There was no simple, quick fix to developing and putting the new programs in place. Exhaustive efforts went in to producing policies, manuals, curriculums,

training schedules, training sessions, performance reviews, in-restaurant QA programs. And, at the same time, the restaurants were open and had to be managed. A hectic couple of years, to say the least, but, in 1987, Clyde's Training Center welcomes the inaugural class. At the end of the day, Clyde's emerged a better organization with solid training programs and a consistent way to manage its business. Clyde's Restaurant Group pressed on with expansion.

JOHN   So, the whole idea of the management training program basically came from the growth of the company forcing a real look at what was important and how the company could be improved. And how management could become more consistent in the way it developed people and therefore how the company could become more consistent in providing service.

   That's eventually how we got the idea that we're going to have to have some kind of standardized way of training people. Not everyone bought into that and we lost some people in the company. We lost four or five people that had been long-term managers because they didn't want to adjust to learning more than one style of management. For them, it was their style of management and that was it. Inconsistency in management is something I've always viewed as being really bad for morale. It was time for a big change.

BEATING THE ODDS MEANS ...

...IF YOU SEE SOMETHING COMING, TAKE REAL ACTION AND DO IT QUICKLY.

JOHN   If our sales go down at all for any protracted period of time, there's something wrong and you have to act quickly. Reassess what you're doing. Start really attacking all your expense things. You're more careful then than you were when times are good. If you see something coming, you have to take real action and you have to do it quickly. Clyde's has been a pretty good barometer of when a recession is starting and when it's ending. We actually made more money in 2008 and 2009 than we ever made before.

No Bigger Than it Needs To Be

John   I think a lot of companies go out and hire people to just hire people. The thought about the organization, though, was that it needed to be simple and no bigger than it needed to be and you add positions when you felt they were necessary, you know, when there was a reason to do it.

My view of my role was to recognize what was necessary and make sure that as we hired corporate management we hired people that were necessary. I never wanted to hire a corporate staff that wasn't absolutely necessary.

Over the years, food and beverage trends, health regulations and escalating customer expectation forced unprecedented necessities on operators. In response, Stuart and John gradually added to the corporate staff but they did so cautiously, always on an "as need" basis.

John   I think just running a business makes it obvious what's necessary in the long run. In other words, if you hire a corporate chef, you should be hiring him because you feel that for consistency sake and innovation you need to hire a corporate chef and so you hire a corporate chef. If you're worried about whether sanitation standards are being upheld, you really need to make sure somebody's there who's making sure those sanitation standards are being upheld in all the restaurants. So we hired a sanitarian. At first though, we grew the corporate organization very slowly, that meant one or two people. I didn't mean like the eight or nine we now have.

It all of a sudden sounds like we hired some giant corporate staff. But we don't have a giant corporate staff. It's virtually no bigger now than it was twenty-five years ago, twenty years ago. We do our own marketing in-house and so we have a marketing director. We have a corporate chef. We have a head of operations, a CFO and a couple of directors of training, one who is actually involved in going out being in the restaurants working with the people in the restaurants rather than being in the training center. And we have a purchasing agent. So, I think today we have only eight or nine corporate personal. Not counting the bookkeeping department.

Yeah, there's no more. Although Sally is Chairman of the Board, that means she does the board meetings but she's not involved in the day-to-day operations. So, it's really not a big corporate structure considering we'll do $135 million maybe this year.

 *INCONSISTENCY IN MANAGEMENT IS REALLY BAD FOR MORALE*

JOHN   As I say, inconsistency in management is something I've always viewed as being really bad for morale. Employees, whether they're waiters, managers or cooks, want to feel they're being treated in a fair and consistent manner. So I think the effort to develop that consistency in terms of the development and treatment of employees led to the management training program. What I really kind of originally liked about the program was it really focused on showing you how and why good businesses were successful, and in teaching you tools for managing people. It kind of showed you what good corporate behavior was and what it could accomplish.

Also, I thought the management training program was a great management training program because it focused on what we were trying to accomplish: the idea of service and value, repeat customers and making the restaurants consistent in terms of service and food and ambiance. And then taking managers and giving them tools to do their job which, when you define it, is doing for employees what employees can't do for themselves. You know, the idea of developing employees, the idea of using consistent management styles for them depending on someone's developmental level. And teaching managers different management styles. No manager can have only one management style. He has to have different styles for different people in different levels of development. Which I thought was really important for people to learn.

The rest of the training was basically built on teaching managers what we expected them to accomplish and giving them the tools to do it.

All of those things really brought a lot of consistency to the company that it hadn't had before. Doing that has made a big impact in the long run on the company about the consistency of the operations and an understanding of what management is and should be.

Beating the Odds Means ...

...A clear understanding of company objectives and the freedom to do what's necessary.

JOHN That's one of the keys in the whole company, to have a clear understanding of what the objectives are, having an understanding of how to meet those objectives, and then being empowered to do what's necessary.

IF YOU DON'T ENFORCE STANDARDS, YOU DON'T HAVE ANY STANDARDS

JOHN What we did basically was establish standards. And then hired people to teach those standards and enforce them. I think that's the critical thought. If you don't enforce standards, you don't have any standards. You don't.

Clyde's has over time always tried on different things. I think it's been a really big part of the company. But at the same time, I think in terms of management and oversight and direction and development, it's something that the company takes very seriously. The whole idea about teaching people what the standards are and making sure that not only do they know what they are but that they're using those standards. It's that kind of loose-tight relationship, where we're loose in that we'll try all kinds of new and different things, but at the same time, we're tight in terms of living up to the standards that we've set for the company.

WORDS TO LIVE BY

"Things never stay the same. They either get better or worse. And part of change is recognizing what your customer wants or what you think your customer wants and be willing to experiment."

John G. Laytham

LET THEM TAKE RISKS. EXPECT MISTAKES

JOHN The whole idea of training in a way is to teach people how to make decisions and then allow them to make them. And they're going to make mistakes. There'll never be a time when there are no mistakes made. Then you got to go in and correct them when they do things they shouldn't be doing.

We've given the chefs more and more freedom. Everyone's going to do the hamburger the same way or a cheeseburger at one of our restaurants, but the chefs now decide probably 60% of what's on the menu and develop their own ideas. The more you get management involved in caring about what they're doing, I think it makes for a much different restaurant.

But there's a lot of thoughtful things that go into providing support. This whole idea about catching people doing something right I find is a really, really positive thing. Or if there was something I don't like, I'll tell him that, too. But to the extent that you can give people a sense of the fact that not only are you happy about the way something went but also that you're happy about the job they're doing making that happen. I think that's part of leadership and I think it's really meaningful for people to be told that they're doing a good job.

And I let them take risks and I let them make mistakes. But at the same time, I am monitoring it all the time and talking to the managers about what's happening. There's nothing wrong with trying as long as you monitor it and you're willing, if it's not working, to do something about it.

SALLY   I feel the same as John. I don't want to say no to ideas that other people in the company want to give a try even though my feeling from the beginning may be this is a bad idea.

JOHN Giving people the opportunity and freedom to try new things, to come up with new procedures they feel would work better, giving people that freedom makes them more creative, makes them work harder, makes them more interested in their job. It's why we have an awful lot of people who've worked in the company for decades.

And that goes all the way, not just through management. It goes through pushing decision-making right down to the level of cooks and waiters. They're the ones who have the right to make a decision if there was a problem with a customer, whether or not we should house their meal or what we should do for them. That whole idea of, "You don't have to go and find a manager. You make a decision." Empowerment gets you away from that "I only work here" kind of mentality. Don't ask me if the customer has a problem. It's your job to take care of it. Empowerment.

I think for the employees that having someone work at helping them develop and become confident gives them a better feeling about themselves and what they do. Better than some-one throwing them out on the floor and saying, "Get at it."

I think it's made the company way more consistent than it was. That's one of the keys in the whole company. To have a clear understanding of what the objectives are, having an under-standing of how to meet those objectives, and then being empowered to do what's necessary.

WHY WE HAVE SO MUCH REPEAT BUSINESS

JOHN That we were training and developing employees, management understood and employees understood what the goals of the company were and that's what they were supposed to be focused on. Before that, they had very little focus. And I think that's the reason we've had so much repeat business over the years. People feel that the restaurants are pretty consistent both in the products they put out and the service they put out.

And it's one of the reasons we spend almost nothing on advertising every year because we have so much repeat business.

GIVING BACK. TOO MANY PEOPLE SIT ON BOARDS AND THEY DON'T SERVE ON BOARDS

GINGER   Stuart and John always had the philosophy that being a good citizen is having a corporate presence in the community and giving back to the community that you are getting so much from. I heard that from both of them in very different ways.

JOHN   Giving back to the community is something that I think started from the very beginning of Clyde's. I don't see how a business can really be successful without being involved in the community.

SALLY   Stuart believed strongly in participating in and giving back to the community and did so in many ways. As did Clyde's.

GINGER   I remember for Clyde's 25th Anniversary Stuart and John decided to give $100,000 to five area charities. That's what Clyde's did for our 25th Anniversary. I cannot think, truly, of a 501(c)3 in Georgetown that has not contacted us for help. Whether it be the Georgetown Senior Center, any one of the parks that have developed public/private partnerships with the city over the years, schools, all kinds of 501(c)3 organizations. They contact us because they see us as being a good corporate citizen. They see Clyde's as being a stable, long-term member of the community that has acted honorably and they would like to reach out to and have our name associated with their organization.
   You can't say yes to everyone. And where you can give a dinner for two or a small donation, you do. But where people are asking for larger, meaningful, particularly cash, contributions and we didn't have that kind of funding, and if it was deemed something that Stuart and John felt was worthy, we would certainly assign someone to help out the organization, whether it was sitting on the board or just help with one fundraiser or whatever. So many of our general managers and corporate managers serve on boards, as does Sally.

SALLY   From the very start, Clyde's supported the arts, like the Washington Opera and other efforts important to the city, like cleaning up the Potomac River through support of American Rivers and Potomac Riverkeeper. And still the giving goes on.

GINGER   So Clyde's concept is to be of service to the community. And one thing I realized early on was that we all felt that too many people sit on boards and they don't serve on boards. So it was very important to all of us that we only take on something that Clyde's could corporately make a difference to and contribute to actively as a corporation.

When Clyde's was asked to have a seat on the Business Improvement District (BID) in Georgetown, I asked Stuart and John, "What do you want me to focus on?" BIDs are formed as the city's tax dollar revenues dwindle but needs grow and basic services are cut. And so Stuart and John said one of the things Georgetown always was left out of was the metro rail system in DC. Georgetown has no metro station. The bus service was inadequate. And if they had cars, workers in the service industry generally couldn't afford parking lots. Street parking was out of the question. So Stuart and John wanted our corporate focus to be on improving transit in Georgetown. The only viable and affordable option was improved bus service. We're not going to take the credit for the improved citywide system, but it was through Clyde's pushing and pushing that we did get the Georgetown metro bus Circulator connection. Because the Circulator system has been so successful, it is now leading to the resurrection of DC streetcars.

Ginger's forte has been since day one as Clyde's liaison to establish and perpetuate effective bi-partisan relationships on all levels with elected city officials and their appointees. In other words, she opens doors.

GINGER   That's what my job was, to have those doors open and ready if we needed to go in. That's what I'm supposed to do. Keep my ear to the ground, keep good relationships with the Mayor's office, with all the Council members in case we needed to go in for a legitimate business reason. Recently John and Tom Meyer had reason to visit with Council members on a business issue. Afterwards, John joked with me, "Well, everyone certainly knew your name and nobody knew my name." That's what my job was, to have those doors open and ready.

Stuart and John were very upfront about how imperative it is to be a good corporate citizen. And that we know who our government leaders are, both locally and on the Hill. Because as a good corporate citizen there were going to be times when we would like to talk to them about matters that affected our restaurants, our industry or our community, small or at large. It was Stuart and John's vision to make sure that we were always corporately connected and had access to people in the proper way, going in with what we considered to be legitimate points of view.

Many organizations approach city officials daily, some with greater luck than others. Clyde's is one of those companies that come forward and officials tend to listen to.

GINGER   Because I don't think we go with unreasonable requests. The Clyde's Restaurant Group is an amazing corporate leader in the city. We have been in the business for fifty years. We have never asked the city for anything that is out of the ordinary. We provide a lot of good, honorable, honest jobs in a very safe environment and contribute millions of dollars in tax revenues.

And Clyde's has never approached community or elected officials with an issue that was strictly of self-interest.

GINGER   No, absolutely. A duality of interests, yes. The transportation issue, for example, to see proper transportation in Georgetown was going to help our employees, no question. But not only our employees but also all of the support staff in the whole hospitality industry, and in the retail, residential, University and hospital communities as well. And, you know, everyone got that right away. I mean, it was just so embraced. This is not self-serving. A duality of interests, yes.
   When there was only Clyde's of Georgetown and the Old Ebbitt Grill, Stuart and John would frequently have breakfast in the Omelette Room – Stuart loved breakfast, could live on breakfast! – and discuss many things and this is how the corporate philosophy about giving to the community developed. It's something that developed then between the two of them because they thought it was the right thing to do. And this concept has not deviated one iota.
   And I don't think it's done anything but stay as solid as it has and benefited every community we're in. Not just Washington, but in Columbia, Maryland and Tysons Corner. Or the Mark Center where we have a lovely barbecue every year for the officers and their families from Alexandria and Arlington who had to respond on 9/11 to the Pentagon. All the Clyde's locations are always involved in their communities. Every one of them.

FIRST IN SOPHISTICATION

Clyde's may have been modeled after the great Hibernian bar, P.J. Clarke's at 55th Street and Third Avenue, NY, but that's where anything even remotely akin to the status quo stops. Clyde's success has been built on original thinking, doing things their way, a sophistication that produced many "firsts" in what was putatively a run-of-the-mill industry.

JOHN There were all kinds of things the company did that were kind of firsts. We were sort of the first place in Washington to hire women on the floor. If you remember back in the old days when Clyde's opened, you never saw a woman working in a bar or a restaurant unless it was the hostess at the Rive Gauche. She was the only one, but you never saw females. At some restaurants you still don't. I find that a good mix of male and female management staff really makes a difference in a restaurant. Women have a better eye for some things, they're much more detailed, and men have a better eye for other things.

We started a profit sharing plan back in 1970.

One of the other things that really changed in that period of time was the idea that people didn't work a million hours a week. And the fact that people worked five-day weeks. They had two days off in a row so they could lead a semi-normal life, not that the restaurant business was ever normal.

We've promoted an awful lot of managers who started as junior managers in the company. We haven't hired an assistant general manager or a general manager from outside the company in twenty years, twenty-five years. So we've actually developed the management we need for expansion within the company, which I think is really positive.

We got rid of having an ad agency and did our marketing either in-house or hired somebody from the outside to help us on individual projects. And that saved a lot of money. It really did save us a lot of money. We have an advertising budget that's less than 1% of our sales and a lot of restaurants have advertising budgets that are 5 or even 10% of their sales.

The company kind of really became much more sophisticated in trying to achieve the goals of the company. We did all kinds of things. We changed it to make goal-setting a big part of management and employees' behavior. There's a real emphasis on doing things well, doing

53

them right, whether it's the food coming out of the kitchen or the service you get on the floor.

We instituted quarterly reviews of all employees, both managers and front and back-of-the-house employees, which we still do today some twenty-seven years later. People are constantly observing people's performance and commenting on it and helping to improve it so that employees and managers theoretically always know where they stand and what you think of their performance. And how their performance can be improved or what you need to do to improve it. I think that whole review system is kind of unusual, that people get quarterly reviews. I mean, I don't think there are many restaurants that do that, or maybe even do reviews, at all, of any kind.

The employee development and training programs. Now instead of having a manager at each restaurant focused on the development of floor staff and that was their primary function at every single restaurant, we opened a training center that did all the basic training of the employees. Then, they were sent back to the restaurant where Top Gun trainers managed the unit training and ran through problems with the new employees. It was very different than having one manager at each restaurant that was basically a hiring and training manager and who wasn't nearly as comprehensive or consistent as it became with the training center.

And, you know, there are a lot of things over the years that we've done that really say we only made things different. In the old days, you try to figure out whether you were over or under budget for what you were scheduling and what it was costing to schedule what you were scheduling. And so we got time machines that had every employee's salary rate in it. Now you could put it in in forty-five minutes or half an hour and hit the one button and it'd tell you whether you were over or under your budget. You could go from there and make the adjustments. There's no real excuse for missing payroll budgets any more. It'll also tell you if you scheduled overtime, which you can get rid of. That was probably one of the most helpful machines we ever bought. Payroll's a big part of the budget.

And we changed the way we did the accounting. We have basically a bookkeeper at each restaurant and then we have like four people who actually do the accounting for the restaurants. But we do all our accounting in-house basically instead of spending more money on outside accounting.

We did all kinds of things. I think it made the biggest change in the company and I don't know too many restaurants that have been around for fifty years or too many restaurant companies who haven't closed a restaurant.

Words To Live By

"Always making things and building things well and doing them the best way possible, spending the extra money but having it right. We certainly got the spending money part right."

John G. Laytham

"You can't do business out of an empty wagon."

Stuart C. Davidson

You Don't Want to Send Bad Fish to Your Biggest Account

JOHN   Another big step we made was hiring somebody to be the purchasing agent for the company. Before that, every chef used to call whoever he wanted to call and order spinach from one guy, potatoes from another guy. Whoever had the cheapest price he would call. And we were all just getting crummy products because nobody wanted to deliver to us because we weren't giving them our whole order.

The whole idea when we changed the purchasing thing was to develop cost-plus contracts and give the one company all of the company business. And so we went from being sort of a horrible customer to a lot of purveyors to being their best customer.   And because we were their best customer, we got the best service and the best quality at a reasonable cost. I mean you don't want to send bad fish or old fish to somebody who is your biggest account.

Now we have cost-plus deals with everybody. And we audit their books at least once a year, maybe twice a year, to make sure we're getting the deal they promised us. They have to show us what they paid for stuff and what they were charged and what they charged us. We have a very reasonable agreement with them that they can still make money and we get the best quality product. Both sides win, you know.

THE SAME PLUMBER FOR 40 YEARS

JOHN I've never tried to beat one of our suppliers. I expect them to be able to make money. I expect to get the best deal that they can afford to give us and make money. But I've never tried to take advantage of any of the people we deal with.

I mean that's one of the things I'm really proud of in the company. We have the same plumber that we had forty years ago, and his family, building all of our plumbing in the company. We have an electrician that we've been dealing with for three decades. We get our meats from the same person we got them from in 1968.

So, Stuart's way of dealing with people like that probably impacted over time my view of dealing with people. We've never tried to take advantage of our suppliers.

BEATING THE ODDS MEANS ...

...DIRE NEEDS NEED OPEN DOORS

GINGER Stuart and John had their open-door policy about people coming to them with problems. And they'd listen no matter who it was in the company, not just management, hourly staff as well. I don't remember anyone who was in dire need ever being turned away.

No More Melons from Another Hemisphere. Or, You Can't Shine Shit

Doing things right meant not compromising on quality, especially when it came to ingredients. Because Clyde's was in the food business and their intent was to consistently serve the best meals possible, it only made sense that they should source the best, the freshest local and native ingredients they could find. Clyde's became zealots in the quest for quality ingredients. Their crusade would have far-reaching, beneficial repercussions on the food supply chain throughout the region.

Tom   Well, we created markets. When we went ahead and started buying and serving locally grown products, we created that market. There was no market for it, you know. No restaurants or hotels in town were doing that. And so we had to go down and kind of access farms.

Most of that product was being sold truck-farm style, kind of roadside down in the country. We would drive down together, Bart and I, and haggle like on the side of the road. I remember there were a couple of days Bart and I would start in DC, drive to Fredericksburg, then drive all the way to the Eastern Shore and back and we'd finish and then deliver everything. So that would take us from five or six in the morning 'til ten or eleven at night. We were meeting a family farmer in a rest stop down somewhere on the Eastern Shore and buying pints of blueberries off the back of his truck. This was the day before cell phones, you know. You're pulling off the road, it's like we're gonna meet this guy at three. We're late and there's no way to call him, you know? What was I on?

And then the next farmers we found by word of mouth. It was like, "Hey, who else has stuff down here?" Or we're driving past farms and stopping and ringing doorbells. It was just one farmer referring other farmers and like that.

In the beginning, all that stuff was sourced out in Westmoreland County. You could drive down to Fredericksburg, hang a left and drive for another hour in that neighborhood. Slowly, we got to the point where we started sourcing stuff also north, a couple of things that gave us more and that also lengthened our seasons. You know, you get a couple more weeks out of strawberries if we start way down south in Fredericksburg.

That product wasn't being wholesaled and so we had to go buy it and handle the distribution ourselves. And so essentially we created a market. We created an outlet for farmers. We start doing it and other people start doing it and farmers say, "Hey, we can make some money growing high quality family farm things 'cause there's a market for it out there."

John We started meeting with local farmers and having them grow things just for us. That started our relationship with Westmoreland Farms and some of the Amish farms and other local growers.

Tom   They ended up planting what we wanted and, as a result, we opened up a market and it made it much more viable for farmers, you know. I mean we were doing that in '86, '87 and it was a good ten years before anybody else kind of jumped on that.

Now it's kind of common, of course. It makes sense, but at the time, I mean, it was a struggle. It turned out it was so much easier to buy a melon from literally another hemisphere. It was way easier to get a melon from Brazil delivered to my restaurant than a melon that was grown sixty-five miles from here. It was a phone call to get a melon from Brazil. It was an all-day-long-in-my-car to get a melon locally.

And you would think it would be cheaper to buy something locally. But no, it cost a lot more money. We would spend an extra $45,000 to $60,000 a summer, a twelve-week season, between the extra money you would pay for the produce and what it would cost to do the shipping ourself. So it was an expense to us but I thought it was well worth it.

John   This was before anybody was doing these kinds of things, including the fancy restaurants that now spend all their time talking about the cheese they go down and pick up wherever.

Tom It was something we could differentiate ourselves with, having real tomatoes and corn and asparagus and strawberries. We made it a real focus of our advertising. So, I think we really opened up that market they call now "farm to table." Now the local wholesalers want to carry it because that's what everybody's asking for.

We did something that is really hard for other people to do and that's why it took so long for them to kind of do it. They didn't see the value in it. The value in it is purely for the customer. I mean, it's really kind of simple. We serve food and if we can't source the best food, I mean, what the hell. I don't care who the chef is, you can't shine shit, you know. You can try to serve the best food but you can't serve the best food and not start out with the best raw products.

I'm not saying we never screw it up after we get hold of it. I'm not going to say that doesn't happen on occasion. But you have to give your chefs a fightin' chance. You give 'em the best.

John That was back when we started buying products directly, whether it was squid or scallops from Nantucket or buying halibut directly from Alaska.

Tom That's another market we kind of started in this area. We sent in 1983, Bill Kohl, at the time the Purchasing Agent for the Ebbitt, to Alaska to source seafood. And that's when we started having wild salmon and halibut drop shipped in from Alaska. The whole salmon farming industry had every chef in the country kind of snookered into believing that farmed salmon was better than wild salmon because it could be controlled. And all the wild salmon was being canned, all of it. I mean, they'd almost give it to you. We'd buy it for less than a dollar a pound. It was all wonderful canned salmon. We discovered that that's a way better fish.

So we started shipping that stuff in thousands of pounds at a time, again, myself or Bart, driving to Dulles Airport. You know, the cargo bins at the remote end of Dulles Airport, loading that goddamned blue truck up and driving all over the beltway. But, in the morning, everybody had like the most beautiful halibut. Halibut used to be a two-day fishing season, or rodeo they called it, and we would buy it for, I don't know, $0.50 a pound or $0.85 a pound. We'd run big specials in the restaurants. Really, really popular.

In the old days, we used to source Nantucket Bay Scallops but they got so popular and so expensive. John would do that. Those were the finest scallops in the world.

JOHN We ordered six tons of squid from Nantucket. People just said I was crazy. I think we went through it in the company in about two months. Twelve thousand pounds of baby squid from Nantucket.

TOM Locally, we would go down and make deals for soft shell crab, lump crabmeat. But that stuff was not unheard of. That was, of course, popular in DC. But unique to us was certainly the halibut and salmon from Alaska. Nantucket scallops, that was unique, and certainly Copper River Salmon.

JOHN Nobody had ever heard of Copper River Salmon when we started bringing it to Washington and now it's the big deal. "We have Copper River Salmon."

TOM We did some crazy stuff. We invested for our own pheasant farm.

JOHN And also we were just kind of disgusted by the fact that all summer we were getting tomatoes from California that were not ripe. We actually paid to outfit three greenhouses to grow us tomatoes in the winter, which just ended up being too expensive to heat the green houses and get tomatoes that were more expensive than the steak they were going with.

TOM Yeah, tomatoes don't want to grow in the winter. And my philosophy after that became like just really embrace the seasons. Like I didn't really feel like eating a tomato salad in February.

But you know, the genesis of all this was that John, when he hired me in '82 or '83, had the concept that we were going to change the menu every day. That really is the genesis of all this and why we do that. It's not because I'm bored in the morning but when products, good stuff, presents itself, you should be able to serve it.

That was considered pretty cutting edge at the time, printing those menus every day. It was like, "Are you crazy? People want consistency. When people come to eat dinner and then when they come back two months later they want the same menu, you know?" And I said, "Well, we'll always have hamburgers but people want good food. They want consistently good food. They don't want consistently mediocre tomato salads. Foolish consistency is the hobgoblin of a simple mind.*

Now it's like everybody from diners to the finest restaurants in town source their produce locally, which is great! Now the local wholesalers want to carry it because that's what everybody's asking for. Well, I can tell you they were not doing that in 1985. I can tell you without question that that was not happening. And anybody that's going to dispute that…. Maybe Jean Louis might have been doing it … but I mean, no. No!

*Tom jousts here with his variation of the pithy jab by Ralph Waldo Emerson, in the essay, "Self-Reliance," from *Essays: First Series* (1841): "A foolish consistency is the hobgoblin of little minds, adored by little statesmen and philosophers and divines."

SPECIAL EVENTS. IN THE SPIRIT OF HAVING A GOOD TIME

"Special events" here does not mean catered events and parties that Clyde's catered on demand. "Special events" means occasions, promotions and celebrations that the restaurants created especially for Clyde's communities.

TOM We had a few when we would want to drum up interest in something. And I'll tell you what I found special events to be like. They really need to have something really special food-wise. In other words, don't throw some lazy party with burgers and hot dogs and pizza. It has to be unique, wonderful food. And there has to be some sort of entertainment that is integral to the event. And an educational component that's like a hook for people. And that's what works for us.

Like while we were pioneering this "farm to table" movement, we said let's have a farm dinner night. We had really cool blue grass music, which I think makes sense with the farm theme, and we had unique, wonderful dishes, something people had not seen. And the educational component, we would bring in the best, brightest of America's chefs that would relate to this type of thing, like Deborah Madison from Greens in San Francisco, the best vegetarian restaurant in the country. You know, Molly O'Neal, the food writer from the *New York Times,* they would come. And that really is a formula that works for special events.

SALLY And we do Oktoberfest and things like that.

Tom   You'll notice our Oktoberfest, we would do wonderful food. And the oompah bands would bring the educational component in with the bells, the horns and explaining about the German traditions, and the dancing and whatnot. People would be mesmerized. But when we throw events that do not fit that format, they're flat.   They fall flat.

Normally, Clyde's special events cannot be classified as one-off, moneymaking parties but rather as perennial ceremonies, community traditions.

Tom   The intention of these things never started out to make money. It was something that was good for the community, good for us. They started out mostly internally for free and then they kind of take on a life of their own.

Sally   I think our single biggest thing is the Oyster Riot. The Oyster Riot is interesting because it was just launched to be a one-time thing and it's become this mega monster, the best party in town. So many people say that.

Tom   Yeah, the first two Oyster Riots were free because nobody was eating oysters. And we wanted to reopen our Oyster Bar 'cause we felt we could do it in a safe way. People didn't trust oysters. People stopped eating them. You need to retrain people. So, what better, we'll throw a party. We'll get people drunk and then they'll eat oysters, you know. So, the first two Oyster Riots were free and even that was hard to get people to go to. Well now it's the biggest party in town. We created a market for oysters when every oyster bar was closed.

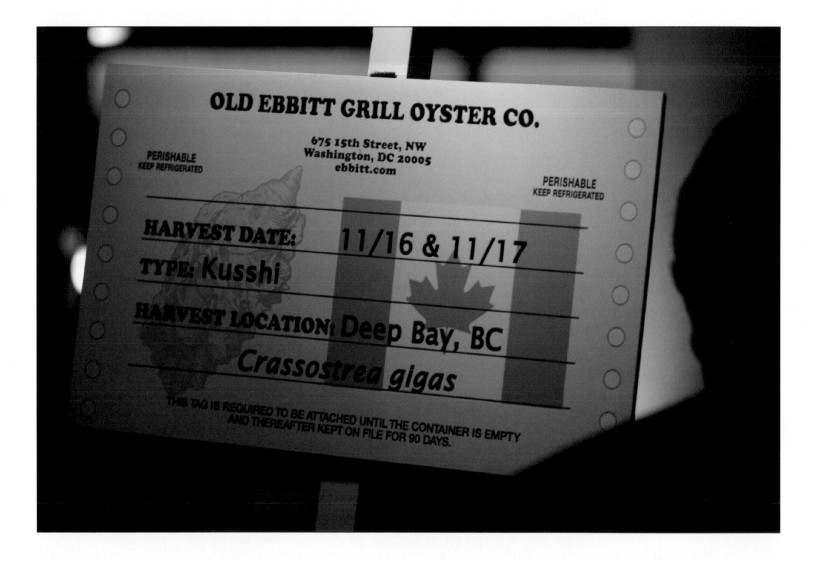

WORDS TO LIVE BY

"Anything worth doing is worth doing well."

Stuart C. Davidson

Beating the Odds Means ...

...Build things that last, that make sense

John   I like building things that last. There's no such thing as a discotheque that lasts, no matter how successful it was. And I like to do things that I know can make sense, and there's no way that a restaurant that's open three or four months a year really can make sense, at least not the way we run restaurants. I just couldn't do a restaurant in a place where I couldn't really make money year around.

EVOLUTION IN HINDSIGHT. WATCHING PEOPLE REACT TO THE THINGS WE'VE DONE

JOHN   I think the company evolved because it became a little more sophisticated and it became better organized and both Stuart and I got very much more involved with design.

But one of the things that I think that has made the evolution thing sort of interesting is watching how people react to the things that we've done. Like at Tysons Corner, when we did that, nobody had ever seen anything quite like Tysons Corner. Whether it was the paintings, whether it was the Art Deco bronzes we got and put in there. And I've just been constantly pleasantly surprised about how interested people are. When we did the Adirondack Lodge, most people had never been to the Adirondacks or seen an Adirondacks lodge. And you know, we have people from the Adirondacks that come there all the time that said they wished they had something like that in the Adirondacks. The woodwork out at the Lodge, the twig work, the fabulous chandeliers that couple did from up in the Adirondacks, they're all over the restaurant. Well, they love it. They love it. "Where did you find a collection like this?"

I just love it when somebody comes into Clyde's that hasn't been here for twenty years or twenty-five years and says, "It's nice to come back and find something that hasn't changed." Because it feels warm and comfortable and it doesn't look shabby and the fact that the bathrooms are way better than they were is a plus but nobody probably remembers what the bathroom was like twenty-five years ago. And the people who are working there are still friendly and courteous, and hopefully the service is as good if not better than it was twenty-five years ago. And I know the food's better. I know how dramatically the menu's changed. The place has been completely redone, and yet people, it still seems the same to them even though it has nothing to do with what it was twenty-five years ago in terms of the menu and the décor and things like that.

A lot of things in the evolution of the company happen that has had to because of a state of mind. I think you have to get over the idea of yourself as the owner and the god-like guy who makes all the decisions. You have to be willing to help people develop and then let them act on their own. And that's where you get the big hits and the big, great ideas.

It wasn't my idea to do deviled eggs with a piece of lump crabmeat on top of each one. But having people use their talents and develop their talents is, I think, critical to being successful rather than trying to micromanage everything yourself.

NOTHING STAYS THE SAME

JOHN   If you think of what Clyde's was forty years ago, there's virtually nothing in Clyde's or that's served at Clyde's that was there thirty years ago. It's true. When I first started working, there were like five things on the menu. And one of them was steak tartar, which I had never had in my life before. And another was a hamburger and a cheeseburger and a New York strip steak and a club steak. And eggs benedict. I think that was the whole menu. And London broil, that was the menu. So, that's how much it's really changed. But it doesn't feel different and I think people want to feel the same, the same kind of warmth and comfortable nature that Clyde's was always about.

   I really believe in that whole axiom. Things are always in a state of change. Things never stay the same. They either get better or worse. And part of change is recognizing what your customer wants or what you think your customer wants and be willing to experiment. I honestly believe that nothing stays the same and that change has to be just constantly ongoing.

FUTURE CLYDE'S

Stuart Carleton Davidson passed away at age 78, from acute myelogenous leukemia in a hospital in Oslo, Norway. An intrepid adventurer, Stuart had traveled north of the Arctic Circle to see polar bears in the wild. His sudden death precipitated organizational shifts in the company nudging ownership and corporate personnel to the threshold of inevitable confrontations.

SALLY Stuart died August 1, 2001. The worst thing that happened was the gaping hole left by Stuart not being there anymore. His personality and his financial background were huge in Clyde's as a company. And he loved the business, and he was so much a part of it. That was something that we couldn't fill.

I inherited the major ownership. Clyde's was a very successful business in town and, from a financial point of view, I would have been better off if I had sold it, which is probably true. In fact, it is true and people knew that. Yeah, it could be sold. My thinking was, of course, quite the opposite. I didn't want to sell. I wanted to see it continue and that's why I spoke to a good number of staff in meetings, "I'm not selling and we are going to continue as we are. I haven't been a part of it from the beginning, but I love it. I love it!" And, no, I had no interest in selling it, even though I was being advised to do so.

But I guess the biggest challenge was, for quite a while, we were all just overwhelmed by Stuart's absence. We couldn't fill his shoes. Nobody could fill his shoes. Me, John, nobody could fill his shoes. So we took a different approach.

Until Stuart's death, Clyde's Restaurant Group had been run by Stuart and John with the support of a lean corporate staff. The board at that time was equally lean consisting principally of Stuart, John and Sally, and so its role was essentially a redundancy of the functions of the company's existing power structure. Stuart's death changed all that.

SALLY I mean, John had been pretty much been in charge of day-to-day everything anyway and he became totally in charge. And the board was new. It's a governing board, not just an in-name board but a governing board. And a lot of thought had already gone into this on Stuart and John's part, that there were people younger already in place who John felt totally comfortable with, that if he and I dropped dead the next day, could run the company.

So, my initial reaction was to reassure everybody that I was not selling. And then my second thought was that I should really form a board that included the key corporate people and bring in Stuart's children, who will eventually inherit my share. The most memorable part of the transition for me? I was very happy that Stuart's children liked the idea of a new board and wanted to become involved, all four of them. And I felt it was a good balance, the family and top corporate management.

TOM Of course, it's frightening. Stuart dies and you have created a board that wasn't there before and it's like any time you put four dogs in a pen, you know, it's like, "Are they gonna want to run the company now? Do they need me, do they like me? Am I gonna be fired? Are they gonna change things? Are they not gonna want to do this? Are they gonna pull all the money out of the company? Are they gonna sell the company?" I mean, you get paranoid, a million things going on in your head.

GINGER John said after the first few board meetings, there developed quickly among the board a great sense of trust for the management team to carry on in the manner in which things were going for fifty years.

TOM They're cool. Honestly, those people are so cool. You could not ask for a cooler situation.

SALLY I mean, nobody in Stuart's family is involved in the day-to-day stuff. Neither am I. Because I founded the board and I'm chairman of the board, I'm a kind of a liaison between staff and family.

Tom   I'd say nothing changed. I think they share their dad's vision. They know what it was and they like Clyde's. They're interested in preserving it and growing it at a responsible and reasonable pace and doing the right things. And doing the right things by the employees like their dad did. I think you could sum it up, they share their father's vision for Clyde's.

Ginger   John said that every single one of the Davidson family members all have great questions.

Tom   They don't mind asking us tough questions, which is what you'd expect of a good board.

Ginger   It's not things we haven't questioned ourselves about, but they all just make you rethink it again. John said it's a great system of checks and balances, a real opportunity for making sure everything is on the table and everything has been reviewed and then covered properly.

Sally   John and I are in constant touch. I mean, he's wonderful about whenever any big decision comes along. He and I discuss things at length before a decision is made. And now that Tom is president, Tom and I talk as well.

Tom   We run past them every big project. We explain what we'd like to do. They sign off on it and they're our biggest cheerleaders. And, you know, they share our pain as well as our successes. When we go through painful times, I feel they're feeling the pain. They're really cool, those people.

Clyde's had expanded over the years really by serendipity, acting on opportunities that had come their way, opportunities that corporate judged to be prudent. With a new board in place, the question now became, "Will the board take a different position on future expansion?"

Tom   I mean, they don't call me and say, "Hey, don't you think it's about time we open another restaurant?" I doubt I would ever get that call. But I'm quite sure if we brought them an opportunity that was carefully thought out and we brought them the numbers and we thought it would work for this and this reason, I'd be very surprised if they would say no to it.

GINGER   Well, there weren't supposed to be any new restaurants and suddenly there was The Hamilton. The Hamilton occurred in the five-year hiatus we were taking and not doing any new projects. But, the opportunity presented itself in what John said he thought was the most prestigious corner in the city. And after discussing it with all the board and making sure everyone knew what we were really getting into, nobody felt it was prudent to walk away from such a good opportunity. That was during the five-year hiatus. So, another new restaurant? I don't guess at that anymore.

SALLY   I don't know how much we should grow. We've really got our hands full. I don't know how many more restaurants we're going to open. I don't know how many we can effectively run. We're pretty big. Maybe John and I differ on this and Tom and I differ on this.

TOM   I honestly don't know. It's like I take the approach of being kind of like an entrepreneur within the restaurant industry. That's a loose description of entrepreneur but, you know, I use entrepreneur and opportunistic. If I see something missing, I like to fill that void. Like when we opened Reston, there was clearly something missing out in Northern Virginia. The same thing with The Hamilton. I thought the whole live music scene was sorely missing in downtown DC. But having said that, developers come to us and they're doing projects. And I think the political landscape is going to change. I think people have to rethink how business is done. And so I honestly don't know right now.

SALLY   I feel there's kind of a limit on what we can effectively manage and run. Each restaurant is complicated, each restaurant needs attention constantly from a maintenance point of view, from a staffing point of view.

TOM   I will say this, I think there's better people in this business now than ever because the restaurant business has been legitimized to some degree finally. When we got into the business, my mother cried when I said I was going to be in the business, you know? It was not cool. And now it's kind of sexy. I mean, one of the reasons we really expanded was simply to give people opportunities to grow. Because if people don't have the opportunity to grow in the company, if they can't go from sous chef to chef, you end up training really good people and staffing the city. So that's another reason to expand.

SALLY   I just don't think it's endless. We have fourteen now, that's a lot. I'd feel better working to improve the restaurants we now have. There is always room for improvement.

Tom I've got a million things roaming around. I think restaurants. I've made my life's work out of it. I remember standing at the corner of that bar at the Old Ebbitt Grill that night we opened. I'm standing next to John and I said to myself, "No matter what happens in my life, you could fire me tomorrow," I said, "I'm gonna be really proud." I knew that restaurant was one for the ages. So that's a hugely important thing to me and I know it is to John.

I don't know if John will verbalize that. John in my mind is all about legacy. I think every move he makes is about legacy, being there. And when he means the long run, he means forever. But the trick is you can't just be there forever, you need to actively be there forever. You can't just say, "We're here for a long time." You have to work at it. You have to renovate, redo, write new menus, do new things, hire new people. That's what's gonna keep you from being just another old restaurant that's tired to a vibrant place that is part of the fabric, culture, history of the town. You know, from a tired old restaurant to a place that's the heartbeat of the city. How's that?

I mean I've always felt we're kind of like chameleons, you know, whatever the market's gonna bear. I'm sure we'll expand some time.

Sally One comment on the kids. I would say that all of them were very happy that I did not want to sell. I mean, who knows, they might. They will own 76% of the company. They will be put in the same situation I was put in. "Do we sell, do we continue?" I mean, we haven't talked about it. I tend to think that most of them, if not all, would like to see us continue, I think.

And that's Clyde's future?

Tom Yeah. To keep it exciting. To keep the vision alive, Stuart's and John's. Just outrageous characters, real men, those guys.

BEATING THE ODDS MEANS ...

...STICK TO WHAT YOU'RE COMFORTABLE WITH.

JOHN We have pretty much stuck to what we do. I've never had a great urge to go and open a chain of Indian restaurants, but that doesn't mean I don't love Indian food, and there are some people who do it very well. And I'd rather go to their place. I think you should do what you're comfortable with.

CLYDE'S RESTAURANT™
G·R·O·U·P

".... the history of Clyde's is both a chronicle of the restaurants and a chronicle of Clyde's corporate policies effectively put to work."

A Brief History of ....

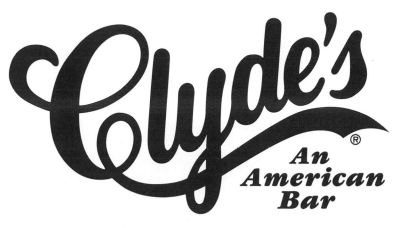

M Street, Georgetown, 1963, was nothing like the commercial, pristine open-air mall it is now, crammed with hip national retailers, swank bath-accessories showrooms and more restaurants than the food court at Mall of America. M Street, Georgetown, 1963, was many degrees darker, a bankrupt east-west egress for federal commuters where derelict warehouses on the south side cast disfigured shadows on the rinky-dink cubbyholes and macerated storefronts on the north. At the west end of M were a couple of grunge bars and cheap places to eat for the less affluent Georgetown student. At night, to the east, there came a slew of Harleys as if out of the manholes at M and Wisconsin. The bikers liked two bars on M Street, the Crazy Horse, a commodious saloon and live-music venue on the north side, and, directly across M Street, the B&J Restaurant, a close and dim, two-room renegade beer joint. The B&J seemed an unlikely place to meet Stuart Davidson, a dapper, tall Harvard grad, a World War II pilot, a Scotsman with the bearing of an eccentric aristocrat.

Also a successful international businessman and Georgetown resident, Davidson enjoyed Manhattan's vogue saloons, a style of bar not to be found in Georgetown during the '60s. The Manhattan bars were urbane neighborhood watering holes serving diners and drinkers who, like himself, believed "it's more fun to eat in a saloon than drink in a restaurant." Disgruntled because Georgetown had no neighborhood bars like those he knew in Manhattan, Davidson decided it was high time it did. The District had relaxed its Blue Laws and the B&J was about to lose its lease and so it was that the natty Davidson was found the summer of '63 scouting the M Street dive drinking beer with a few burley bikers. Davidson leased the joint, renamed it

Clyde's, after the River Clyde in Scotland, opened the doors in August, and at that instant, set in motion an enterprise that would literally leave its indelible stamp on the DC metro area bar scene for years to come.

Little known to Davidson at the time he leased the B&J space, there was a prep school senior getting ready to leave home to go to college in Washington, DC, the affable young man destiny had chosen to be Davidson's partner in the steady, meteoric rise of the Clyde's Restaurant Group.

Georgetown University, Georgetown, fall 1963, saw a slender, cerebral freshman from near Pottstown, PA walk on campus. John Laytham had come to study foreign relations at Georgetown's distinguished School of Foreign Service. A bright, ambitious student, Laytham settled in to the academic program then went in earnest search of a part-time job ostensibly to earn "spending money," which in translation meant, "I needed cash for dates." Laytham took a dishwasher job at Clyde's, which Davidson had opened six months earlier, and so the Georgetown freshman became an employee of a company he would never leave. Over the years, Laytham worked his way rung by rung to become general manager, then, in 1968, Davidson offered him a buy-in as a sole partner.

It was Laytham who concocted the brilliant bright idea – perhaps the single most important stroke of genius in Clyde's history – that would not only give him the bartender shift he desperately wanted but also rocket Clyde's above its M street competition and seal Clyde's place as DC's preeminent saloon operation in the years to come. What was Laytham's brilliant idea? *Open for Sunday brunch.* Sunday brunch is now a mainstay for many saloons, but this was not the case in Georgetown when Laytham brainstormed the idea. The novelty of Sunday

brunch in DC was one thing; it was another to serve an exceptional brunch menu, something Laytham insisted on. In the late '60s and early '70s, saloon menus were pretty much restricted by whatever amateur short-order cooks could grill, fry or sandwich. The quality of Clyde's menu as well as the preparation of its dishes set Clyde's apart; the M Street saloon soon became famous for its burgers and zesty chili, then omelettes, and ultimately Clyde's own brand of American regional cooking, featuring fresh, local ingredients and wholesome, creative treatments of classic culinary staples, each dish overseen by professional chefs and cooks. Great food done well each and every time. Food became Clyde's differentiator,

a pivotal element in Clyde's history and growth, an empire born of a Sunday brunch.

CLYDE'S FRENCH TOAST 4.25
    made with Vie de France bread
STEAK SANDWICH 6.95
STEAK and EGGS 5.95
EGGS BENEDICT 5.25
EGGS FLORENTINE 4.95
CLYDE'S HOMEMADE QUICHE 5.25
    Lorraine or Spinach & Mushroom
EGGS, any style 3.85
EGGS w/HAM, BACON or SAUSAGE 4.75
Q's OMELETTES, Choice of Two Fillings 4.75
    Onion, Tomato, Mushroom,
    Ham, Sausage, Bacon, Swiss or American Cheese

    SIDE ORDERS: Bacon 1.25
                       Ham or Sausage..... 1.50

    all brunch items include salad and rum bun
         Bleu Cheese Dressing .50 extra
BOOKER T's SOUTHERN SUNSHINE 1.25
    Orange juice, squeezed daily

CLYDE'S FAVORITE BRUNCH LIBATIONS

MIMOSA—
    Booker T's Southern Sunshine and Champagne
MAY PUNCH—
    Champagne, May Wine and a Brandied Strawberry
THE BLOODY MARY—
    Sacramento Tomato juice, a fine selection of spices,
    Gordon's Vodka, Garnished with Citrus
KIR—
    French Country White Wine with a splash of Black
    Currant Liqueur
THE SCREWDRIVER—
    Sweet with Orange Juice or
    Tart with Grapefruit Juice
CHAMPAGNE, by the glass

CLYDE'S FAMOUS CHILI
(Serves Six to Eight)

Sweet and slightly hot, this saloon-style chili with beans has been a staple on Clyde's menu for over forty years. Liz Taylor would order it by the gallon and have it shipped to her house! Since we no longer offer our chili in the can at Britches clothing store, it's only fair that we give you the recipe that has been top secret for many years.

1 tbsp	vegetable oil
1 lb.	pound small diced onion
1 tbsp	minced fresh garlic
1 1/2 lbs	ground beef
1	25-ounce can chili beans
1	12-ounce jar chili sauce
2 tbsp	light chili powder
1/4 cup	dark chili powder*
2 tblsp	Worcestershire sauce

1. In a heavy bottomed pot, saute the onion and garlic in the vegetable oil until golden brown.
2. Add the beef to the onions and cook until it is about medium-rare. Do not stir the beef around too much - you want to have some large clumps of beef in the finished chili.
3. Add the rest of the ingredients and stir until it is just blended. (It may seem like a lot of powder but that's why they call it chili!)
4. Cook the chili over medium heat for about 10 minutes, just until the meat is fully cooked. Don't overcook it!

Serve the Clyde's chili with ice cold beer and condiments like shredded sharp cheddar cheese, sour cream and minced onions.

*The light chili powders have more of the hot seeds or flakes ground with the pods. By using more of the dark powder our chili is a little sweeter. If you can't find light chili powder, just using a little bit extra of the dark powder will taste great.

Up until Stuart Davidson's demise in 2001, the history of Clyde's has been the history of the relationship between Davidson and Laytham. The two men brought different but equal skills, sensibilities and perspectives to the business. Davidson's concept of the neighborhood saloon ("It's more fun to eat in a saloon than drink in a restaurant.") is still the cornerstone of Clyde's unique approach to the saloon business, an approach ersatz saloons have copied and benefited from. Laytham's ability to manifest Clyde's differentiated saloon concept through the F&B operation, exceptional customer service and professional management practices has been peerless, his acuity, instincts and creative intuition on par with genius. What's telling about the history of the relationship between Davidson and Laytham and the history of the Clyde's organization is this impressive fact: In spite of the blistering vulnerability (that's PC for "high mortality rate") inside the restaurant industry, of the fourteen restaurants Clyde's has opened since 1963, all fourteen are still open and the company flourishing.

Clyde's of Georgetown, August, 1963, the story of the mother ship has been told. However, as epilogue, Davidson and Laytham shut down Clyde's of Georgetown in 1996 for structural restoration and a decorative makeover. Some things are sacred to a saloon and cannot be regarded as dispensable. High on the list of indispensables is the saloon's bar. While walls were knocked down, floors torn up, booths installed, ceilings replaced, bathrooms redone, a lovely French limestone fireplace bolted in, aircraft and sporting memorabilia hung, the old kitchen replaced with a much larger one, Clyde's original oak bar stood its ground, a solid icon of Clyde's heritage and the place from which all other Clyde's bars hail.

OLD EBBITT GRILL®
Since 1856

The Old Ebbitt Grill, 1970, DC's best saloon operator purchases DC's oldest saloon…for a song and a stein! The Old Ebbitt Grill, Washington's oldest saloon, has been traced back through numerous downtown addresses to a stand-around bar in a boarding house bought by innkeeper William E. Ebbitt in 1856. As the old Old Ebbitt (and its presidential patrons) migrated successively westward from what is now Chinatown toward a prestigious address at F and 15th Streets a block from the White House, it lugged a congeries of historical memorabilia and beer steins along with it.

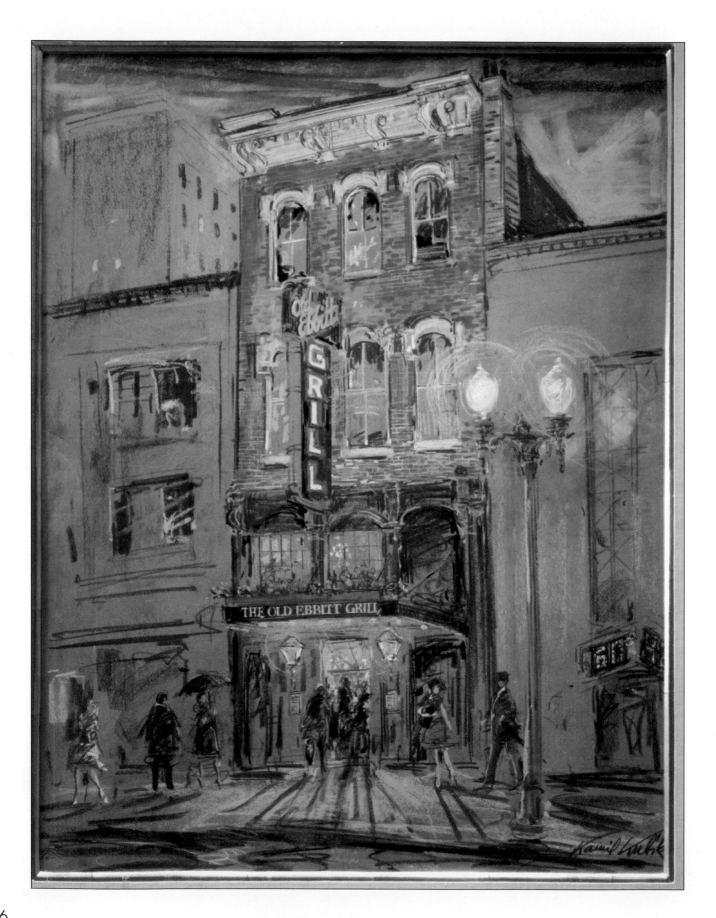

Spiraling on hard times in the '60s and in arrears on taxes, the Ebbitt shuts down. Davidson and Laytham get wind of the tax auction and head downtown hoping to pick up the chandeliers, the stein collection and maybe a stuffed animal or two that Teddy Roosevelt was said to have bagged. A couple of hours and $11,200 later, the Clyde's owners walk away with the stein collection and the rest of the business thrown in for good measure. One more relocation and a massive expansion thirteen years later lands the Old Ebbitt Grill at its current location directly across from the U.S Treasury at 675 15th St. The Ebbitt is a welcome pandemic in the neighborhood expanding its dining rooms and bars to adjacent spaces and the Ebbitt Express carryout into the interior corridors. The Old Ebbitt Grill isn't only the oldest saloon in DC; it's also the busiest. For the past several years, at moderate price points, the Old Ebbitt Grill has ranked among the top-grossing restaurants in the country.

Clyde's of Columbia, Columbia, Maryland, 1975. For the first time, Clyde's shuttles its neighborhood bar concept to a neighborhood outside Washington, DC. Testing the waters at this lakeside community in Columbia, Maryland was something Davidson and Laytham approached with trepidation.

Only forty miles but it might as well have been four thousand for a city-bred independent restaurant company that liked to hold its assets close to its chest. "Nervous-making" was how Laytham described it. But, by now Clyde's had cache in the region and Columbia's developers hoped to capitalize on Clyde's reputation. They offered the two partners the proverbial deal to venture out of DC. After a jittery opening, management regrouped and it was clear sailing from then on out as Clyde's of Columbia became the community's local saloon and restaurant. Encouraged by this success, Davidson and Laytham christened Clyde's Restaurant Group (CRG) with an eye toward developing neighborhood-centric saloons throughout the DC metro area.

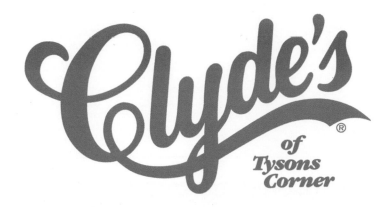

Clyde's of Tysons Corner, Tysons Corner, Virginia, 1980, a 21st century Virginia roadhouse built in the grand tradition of the great American Art Deco roadhouse, copper roof included. Clyde's first crack at behemoth: 450 seats, four dining rooms four menus, two public bars including Clyde's first open platform island bar, two kitchens, a second-floor in-house catering facility with balconies overlooking two live palm trees dropped by crane into in-ground planters in the center of an atrium dining room. The décor and furnishings are nothing short of opulent, commissioned bawdy satyric murals, bold avian paintings, Art Deco statuettes, rich woods, brass table lanterns, lush leather custom chairs and banquettes, contemporary stain-glass panels and bar shelving, terra cotta tile flooring. The Tysons roadhouse is extravagance, a horn-of-plenty born of necessity: the building crowns a bluff above the crossroads connecting Washington, DC and most of Northern Virginia, the largest targeted neighborhood in Clyde's history, stretching from Georgetown to Leesburg.

The 1789 Restaurants, Georgetown, Washington, DC, 1985, was CRG's first bona fide turnkey, the resuscitation of three legendary, albeit wilting, Georgetown restaurant and club venues dating back to the 1960s: the fine dining 1789 Restaurant, the popular Hoya rathskeller The Tombs, and the Art Deco nightclub F. Scott's. The idea behind the takeover: preserve the identities of the three brands but renovate the facilities, services and products. But first, shore up the building, which included a colossal rehab of the foundation of the mid-1800s Federal townhouse and the buildout of new kitchens. Laytham traded out the 1789's French cuisine for an upscale American regional menu rooted in classical culinary traditions, and introduced a modified northern Italian menu at F. Scott's, which today functions as a glamorous space for private events. Keeping a casual American menu, The Tombs could only benefit from Clyde's pedigree.

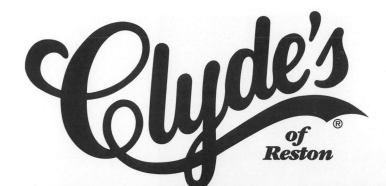

Clyde's of Reston, Reston Town Center, Reston, Virginia, 1991, was a "must win" opening for CRG. On the heels of a long period of economic recovery and expansion – a period of growth real estate developers capitalized on by financing planned communities and town centers such as Reston — came the agonizing, global recession of 1990 and 1991. The service sector, along with the white-collar workers employed by these businesses, took the brunt of the downturn. The threat to new businesses in burgeoning markets such as Reston was terrific and real. Not good timing for Clyde's at Reston. The company was caught in the thick of building and staffing a new restaurant. Clyde's of Reston had to be done right from ground zero, day one.

Historically, the opening of Reston was the first real test of the corporate-wide fiscal, management, product, service and training systems CRG had developed from the mid '80's on. Clyde's response to the '91 recession was to confront the threat head on using the tactics from its newly developed corporate programs: offer an attractive, friendly ambiance, serve great American food and drink, give quick, professional customer service, honor customer requests, guarantee hands-on management, offer unbeatable value for the dollar, control costs, and deliver the basics consistently, first time, every time, customer by customer. Clyde's of Reston was well oiled by the time the first customer walked through the revolving door. Reston was an instant hit, a recession buster! In hindsight, Reston reassured Clyde's Restaurant Group that its strategy for systems development and unit expansion was credible and working.

The Tomato Palace

The Tomato Palace, Columbia, Maryland, 1993, happened because a travel agency next door to Clyde's of Columbia lost its lease. John Laytham jumped on the vacant space in a move to block any competing restaurant from taking it over. But what to do with a space about the size of the kitchens at Clyde's of Tysons Corner? Simple. Put in a small exposition kitchen, outfit the dining room with family-size booths, lease the sidewalk out front for a 50-seat lake-view café, make the place kid friendly, station a couple of waitresses dressed up in plum tomato body suits outside to draw in Columbia's many families, then crank out homemade pizzas, pasta dishes, fresh salads and a few southern Italian entrees. Easy. Clyde's first foray into whimsical family dining.

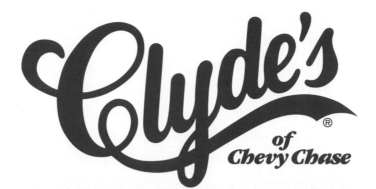

Clyde's of Chevy Chase, Chevy Chase, Maryland, 1995, was the last restaurant designed by the late John Richards Andrews, the independent who had over the years become known throughout the city as "Clyde's architect." Andrews, Davidson and Laytham introduced design features at Chevy Chase that made it unique in Clyde's history. Most notably, it was the first time the main bar had been separated physically – in this case, placed on a different floor – from the main dining rooms, a real architectural departure for this venerable saloon operator whose MO has always been "It's more fun to eat in a saloon than drink in a restaurant." While this change represented an architectural digression, not so conceptually. Conceptually, Clyde's has always been about serving the neighborhood, and the community in Chevy Chase could not have been more disparate; on one hand were well-heeled, conservative elders and on the other, fun-loving, single professionals. The other unique design element here actually addressed the polarization in the community makeup by using décor to bring the two extremes together: Andrews and Clyde's two partners designed and decorated the interior around a storied theme, the story being "yesteryears' travel." The main dining room recreates a passenger train car modeled after the luxurious accommodations of the transcontinental Orient Express; the Travel Room pays homage to early transatlantic steamship and air travel. To the delight of kids, a model locomotive races along train tracks suspended from the ceiling.

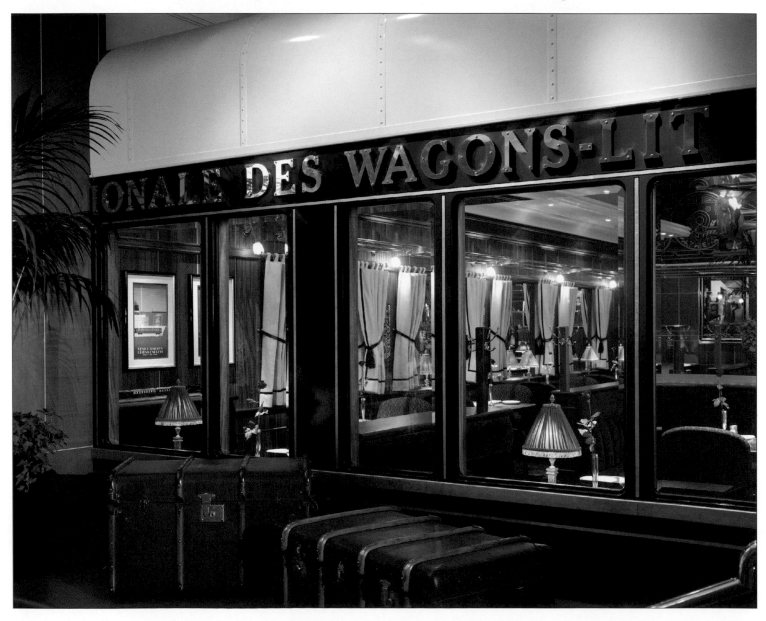

Downstairs is the huge island Race Bar, a lounge and concealed stage. Take that back! Downstairs is a racecar museum with bar attached; Clyde's put several antique exotic sports cars on exhibit throughout the Race Bar, hence the name. It is at the Race Bar that the racier element of the community meet, eat, drink, play and dance to live music.

In 2005, the Chevy Chase Center reinvented itself as a top-of-the-line Main Street, the construction forcing Clyde's to close temporarily. Clyde's used the opportunity to refurbish, then reopen as a stand-alone building. Reinvigorated as an attraction in the chic Chevy Chase Collection, Clyde's rubs elbows with Gucci, Tiffany, Ralph Lauren, Cartier, Jimmy Choo and other stylish chichi. Not bad company for a Georgetown saloon hailing from the '60s!

Clyde's at Mark Center

Clyde's at Mark Center, Alexandria, Virginia, 1998. For years Clyde's toyed with the idea of opening a bar and restaurant in Alexandria, VA, to the point of purchasing Old Town's historic Old Club Restaurant (once a clubhouse for George Washington and friends). The Old Club project fizzled out but Clyde's persisted in historic Alexandria's West End, opening Clyde's at Mark Center thirty-five years after Davidson unlatched Clyde's on M Street. Clyde's had by now perfected a signature menu that worked for the Clyde's customer: lots of dishes to choose from, substantial, straightforward recipes and preparations using fresh, seasonal ingredients, and produce supplied preferably by local farmers and regional suppliers. The marching order in the kitchens went something like, "Great meals start with great ingredients. Don't mess it up playing with the food." In 1998, nothing-short-of-the-best customer service was still a mantra as was impeccable ambiance, but the storied theme interior of Chevy Chase had now morphed into habitats! Fans of all things water, Davidson and Laytham, with their posse of devil-may-care designer friends, squeezed five fabricated habitats into Mark Center's three dining rooms and two bars, each one memorializing sporting life on the water: an Adirondack fishing camp, a Chesapeake Bay hunt club, a Potomac boathouse, Newport yacht and a Nantucket beach shack cum bait and tackle shop — gloriously outfitted in the way only Clyde's can!

Tower Oaks Lodge, Rockville, Maryland, 2002, carries on CRG's experiment with building habitats in the restaurants. Overlooking a 21-acre nature preserve, Tower Oaks Lodge could be one of the Adirondack stone and timber "Great Camps" built in the late 1800s at Raquette Lake, NY. Actually, the Lodge stretches out around a 200-year old, two-story timber barn brought down from Vermont, the outlying rooms and bars embellished by stone and wood construction.

Clyde's scoured the Adirondacks for art and artifacts to give the Lodge its Adirondack authenticity. Certainly, experimenting with the design, decoration and ambiance of the restaurants is a labor of love for Laytham. It's what he lives for. But there is more to it than that. Creating unique environments for the customer is, when all is said and done, a no-brainer in Clyde's evolving competitive corporate culture: if creating environments-as-ambiance can enhance the customers' experience, if it boosts perceived value at no cost to the customer, then do it. Customer reviews of Tower Oaks Lodge support this edict; extravagant kudos about the luxury and homey comfort of the Lodge often include this surprise: "affordable prices." Tower Oaks Lodge makes it clear that the history of Clyde's is both a chronicle of the restaurants and a chronicle of Clyde's corporate policies effectively put to work.

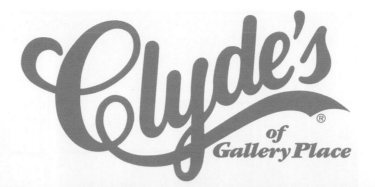

Clyde's of Gallery Place, Washington, DC, 2005, brings Clyde's back home, the first Clyde's inside Washington's city limits since 1970. True to form, Clyde's homecoming was sensational. A two-level restaurant, four bars, five dining rooms, a raw bar and a private dining room. Located in the renewed Penn Quarter just a block or two away from the Verizon Center and Chinatown's colorful Friendship Gate on 7th Street, this Grand Victorian saloon, fashioned after the regal and opulent style of Hong Kong's Empire Era, reminds the city that Clyde's does saloon better than anyone. Open as many as seventeen hours a day and serving food until 1:00 am, Gallery Place approximates the legacy that saloonkeepers, the Clyde's of the city, rarely close their doors.

131

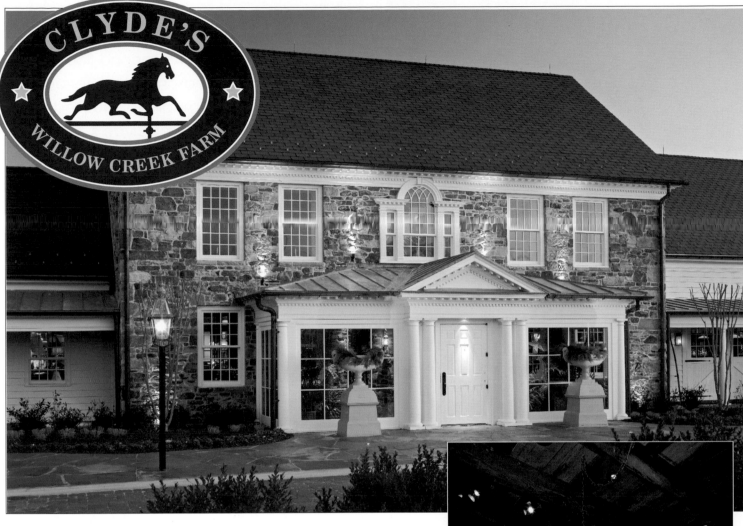

Clyde's Willow Creek Farm, Broadlands, VA, 2006, thirty miles northwest of Georgetown in verdant Loudoun County, opened as a restaurant, bar, conference and catering facility to serve the wellspring of IT and telecommunications companies and the communities that grew up in support of those companies near Dulles Airport. The American country tavern was built with the materials of four 18th and 19th-century buildings from Vermont and Virginia: the Samuel French Tavern (c. 1804), the Chandler Barn (c. 1885), the Roxbury House (c. 1810), and the Richmond House (1780), each of which Clyde's Restaurant Group purchased, disassembled, indexed and put in storage for as many as twenty

years. The result, a sprawling, rustic, stately tavern and dining multiplex that Includes seven dining rooms, four bars, two second-floor private dining rooms, a seasonal arbor Terrace and the snuggest bar imaginable tucked into a quaint outbuilding. Par for Clyde's, the interior is inviting and comfortable, stunningly decorated with original artwork, sculpture, historic artifacts and an over-the-top collection of museum-quality 18th-century horse-drawn carriages, most strung from solid timber struts.

Clyde's commitment to cooking with locally grown produce and ingredients hits zenith at Willow Creek. Outback is an organic, raised-

bed farm supplying the ultra-modern kitchen with the fruits, vegetables, herbs, seasonings and honey that go from garden to plate. Going Green is nothing new at Clyde's. Truth of the matter is, the Green trend has finally caught up to Clyde's.

The HAMILTON®

EAT · DRINK · LISTEN

The Hamilton opened downtown Washington, DC, in December 2011, just around the corner from the Old Ebbitt Grill. That The Hamilton might steal business away from the Ebbitt initially raised some eyebrows. John Laytham was unruffled: "It's a conscious attempt to make the new place different than the Old Ebbitt but, at the same time, just as sophisticated and interesting…but different."

Interesting and different, The Hamilton is a radical concept for DC's pre-eminent restaurant/saloon titan. To call The Hamilton a 37,000-square-foot "bazaar" would not be inappropriate. Spread over multiple levels, The Hamilton shows the opulent, tried-but-true restaurant and saloon amenities Clyde's has become famous for; but new to The Hamilton are innovative menu offerings, such as house-made charcuterie, a stand-alone, sit-down sushi concession, and, downstairs, a state-of-the-art live music entertainment venue. Tucked away quietly upstairs is the intimate "Loft" lounge, a secluded miniature version of the grand, boisterous saloons on the main floor.

The Hamilton floor plan exploits the expansive, tiered concourse in what was once Garfinckels department store, DC's Bergdorf Goodman in the early to late 1900s. Clyde's American Bistro, the central 800-seat restaurant and bar space, has been carved into smaller rooms to sift the high-volume, high-energy crowd into different environments, basically the same principle that drives multiplex cinemas: different shows for different audiences. The Bistro accommodates several bars and features nearly two dozen micros-brews and draft beers. The mezzanine "Loft" doubles as a 45-seat private dining room and bar. Walking through the multiplex, the strategy behind The Hamilton becomes clear: transform the corner of 14th and F NW into a dynamic entertainment micro-District.

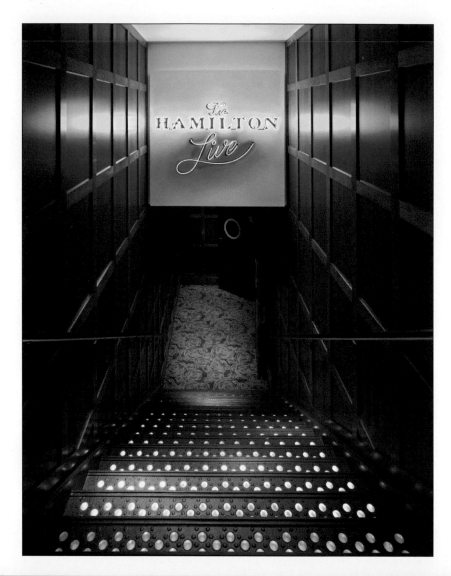

J. Garrett Glover is a management consultant specializing in the restaurant business. Formerly Clyde's first corporate operations manager, Garrett has over 45 years of experience in the hospitality industry. In addition to his work for Clyde's, Garrett's clients include independent restaurant companies, government agencies, and economic development agencies. He is the author of restaurant trade articles, white papers, management, human resource, and service manuals. Garrett has produced independent documentaries and TV specials for the Food Network.

A native Washingtonian, Garrett holds degrees from Georgetown University, The Catholic University of America, and a Ph.D. from New York University. He has taught at Columbia University in New York and The Corcoran College of Art in Washington, DC. He lives with his wife and two children outside Washington, DC on an historic tobacco farm with its patent tract dating back to 1661.

For sales, editorial information, subsidiary rights information
or a catalog, please write or phone or e-mail
Brick Tower Press
1230 Park Avenue
New York, NY 10128
Sales: 1-800-68-BRICK
Tel: 212-427-7139
www.BrickTowerPress.com
email: bricktower@aol.com

www.Ingram.com

For sales in the UK and Europe please contact our distributor,
Gazelle Book Services
Falcon House, Queens Square
Lancaster, LA1 1RN, UK
Tel: (01524) 68765 Fax: (01524) 63232
stef@gazellebooks.co.uk